previously
I Know You Love Me and Y...

GETTING THE LOVE
YOU DESERVE

STEFAN DEUTSCH

THDC Press | New York

THDC Press; www.thdc.org.

PRINTING HISTORY
First edition / March 2014
I Know You Love Me and You Know I Love You: Fulfill the Promise of Your Marriage Vows / Copyright © 2014 Stefan Deutsch. Edited and designed by Emily Wilson.
Second edition / September 2015
Cover design by Patrick Sheegog and Stefan Deutsch. Book interior edited and designed by Lisa Hosokawa Garber.

The material in this book cannot substitute for professional advice; further, the author is not liable if the reader relied on the material and was financially damaged. All stories shared are recalled to the best of the author's knowledge. All clients' names and other identifying details have been changed to protect their privacy.

ISBN 978-0-9916283-1-5

18 17 16 15 14   2 3 4 5 6

In memory of my mother, Aliz Katz Deutsch, born in 1921, the tenth child of a family she lost, almost entirely, to the Holocaust. Before I learned what unconditional love was, I experienced it from this patient, kind, thoughtful, giving, encouraging person. Her blessed nature inspired my search for the solution to end hate, anger, and emotional pain in the world. My work will continue until my last breath as a tribute to her life and her legacy of unconditional love.

01101100 01101111 01110110 01100101 01101100 01101111 01110110 01100101 01101100 01101111

CONTENTS

01101100 01101111 01110110 01100101 01101100 01101111 01110110 01100101 01101100 01101111

01101100 01101111 01110110 01100101 01101100 01101111 01110110 01100101 01101100 01101111

ILLUSTRATIONS AND EXERCISES

01101100 01101111 01110110 01100101 01101100 01101111 01110110 01100101 01101100 01101111

01101100 01101111 01110110 01100101 01101100 01101111 01110110 01100101 01101100 01101111

FOREWORD

01101100 01101111 01110110 01100101 01101100 01101111 01110110 01100101 01101100 01101111

We all want love. And we all need love to thrive and even survive. Yet, many people are starving for it and frustrated in their inability to get it. Stefan Deutsch offers us a clear path to bring more love into our lives.

As Stefan explains, love is a nutrient as necessary as oxygen, food, and water. If you love someone, you would not want to deprive them of the air they breathe. Why would you want to deprive them of your love?

The reasons people deprive each other of love are many, but they're mostly rooted in ignorance and protection from pain. Stefan Deutsch educates us on what love is, how to rise above our fears, and how to consciously choose to love unconditionally. Vision is the guidepost. He urges us to create a vision of the unconditional relationship we want and communicate it to our partner. So, together, we are inspired toward that endeavor.

A story best explains the power of vision.

Two people were working side by side laying bricks. One was grunting and cursing in a kind of hurried frenzy, while the other was serene, calm, and humming softly. A passerby observing these two workers was perplexed. How could two people with the exact same job approach it so differently? The passerby asked what they were doing. The irritated worker said, "That's a silly question; I'm laying bricks." The other worker said with a smile, "I'm building a cathedral."

It turns out that having a vision transforms one's experience of the world. Such is the power of Stefan's message to us. In a warm and practical way, he lays out an exquisite blueprint of his vision of unconditional love with specific instructions for building our own love cathedral.

Stefan and I first met as psychotherapists with our own radio talk shows, exchanging guest spots on each other's broadcasts. I was immediately impressed by his keen wit, intelligence, exuberance, and passion for educating people about the true nature of love. Since he was Hungarian, I also related to him from my Hungarian ancestry. The majority of his family had been murdered by the Nazis, and later, he and his parents fled the Communists. I met his wife, Elsa, and found another kindred spirit. Together, with my husband, Spence, we spent many delightful hours in excited conversation about Stefan's theory of the power and creation of unconditional love.

Over the years, I have observed Stefan implement his four-pronged theory of awareness, vision, communication, and loving behavior for couples and individuals with very successful results.

In 2013, Barbara L. Fredrickson presented scientific evidence providing proof for Stefan's master theory in her book *Love 2.0*. It was only then that he was able to place the final brick in his own cathedral. In *Love Decoded*, he has shown himself to be an architect par excellence, offering the hope of true and lasting love and the joy of actually achieving it.

Stefan's message of giving and receiving love is even more poignant knowing his extraordinary legacy of tragedy. At the end of her diary, Anne Frank concluded that people are really good at heart.

Stefan Deutsch has transcended his own pain to be able to love unconditionally and to equip people with the tools they need to manifest good-heartedness in the world.

I am deeply gratified to introduce Stefan Deutsch to you. He lives what he says. Stefan is a lover in the fullest sense of the word, bringing love to his family, friends, colleagues, students, audiences, and people in the wide world.

Yes, love is a palpable nutrient there for the choosing. It can be yours. Just open these pages and take the steps with your partner on your own unique journey. Go with Stefan as he guides you on the path to a fuller and richer life. You will be very happy you did.

Duffy Spencer, PhD, LMHC, *is a psychotherapist and social psychologist who speaks, trains, and coaches individuals and groups to overcome inner obstacles for their highest success.*

PREFACE

A t a very young age, I began to learn what real fear was and what hatred could do to people. My parents survived the Nazi extermination camps. After the war, my family and I fled the Soviet-instated Communists in Hungary, spending a year in an Austrian refugee camp before arriving in America.

With this background, I decided very early in life that my mission would be to find ways to help make the world a better and more loving place.

After graduating college, I spent some time teaching underserved children with the NYC Board of Education. I later did some study in movement therapy at NYU Graduate School and then founded an organization called Impact on Hunger, which became the educational umbrella arm of the US hunger community, including UNICEF. I was featured on CNN, spoke to thousands of people at major league sports venues, produced shows with celebrities like Jeff Bridges, and with an AID grant created the first K–12 curriculum guide to ending hunger. It felt good to be making a real difference. It was this last experience of working to eliminate starvation that opened the door to my current work and led to a critical discovery.

One of the things I noticed in my exploration of human development and behavior was that all of us feel deeply hurt whenever we are treated unlovingly or when love is withheld from us. *Why does it hurt so much?* I began asking myself. *Why don't we tell people that we need them to be more loving? Why aren't we always loving to others?*

These questions came alive for me. When I wasn't busy with tasks that needed my immediate attention, I would find myself looking back at them and raising even more questions. *What is love, really? What is loving behavior? How can we get it and give it consistently and unconditionally? Why is that so difficult? Why aren't we more loving to ourselves?* That's the short version.

In time, I began to formulate answers and develop ideas. One of my earliest and most important theories was that love is an essential life-sustaining energy that nourishes us, just like air, food, and water. Thirty years later, this finding was finally scientifically validated.[1]

This explains why we need love. Without it, we wither. With it, we thrive. Although everyone is capable of giving love, most of us have a great deal of difficulty giving it consistently. The reason for this is that most of us were never taught how to give and get love consistently and unconditionally. These ideas are so infrequently discussed or studied that most of us have a hard time articulating what love is!

Continuing to witness a relentless stream of prejudice, hate, and violence everywhere, I realized that there was another cause to all this strife, a much less understood hunger that was ravaging our planet. This was our hunger for love. Our global citizenry is literally malnourished in a way we haven't begun to talk about.

Ever since this realization, I have researched ways to address this other hunger and eliminate it by informing as many people about it as possible.

---

1. Barbara L. Fredrickson, *Love 2.0: How Our Supreme Emotion Affects Everything We Think, Do, Feel, and Become* (New York: Hudson Street Press, 2013).

After more than thirty years of developing my ideas, applying them in my clinical practice, and teaching them to colleagues, I decided to bring the idea of love as nourishment to a larger audience. You are holding the result of that decision, and I hope you will find this book as satisfying and challenging to read as it was for me to write.

The ideas within this book and their application have changed lives. Perhaps they will change yours, as well.

01101100 01101111 01110110 01100101 01101100 01101111 01110110 01100101 01101100 01101111

ACKNOWLEDGMENTS

01101100 01101111 01110110 01100101 01101100 01101111 01110110 01100101 01101100 01101111

This book is the culmination of my lifelong search for answers about man's inhumanity to man and what can be done about it. As such, it has been a labor of love. There were many times when I wondered, *What am I doing, trying to heal the world?* The answer was always the same: *That is what I was given to do, and I must proceed.* I want to acknowledge my many clients, everyone who attended a workshop or lecture or listened to my radio program. It was your continual enthusiasm for what you learned and the amazing results you achieved that motivated me to carry on writing.

I want to give a special thanks to my wife, who has patiently listened to my ideas about love and human development and supported them for decades. Turning our home into an office and infringing on her privacy was a huge sacrifice, but she allowed me to make this part of my journey easier.

I also want to acknowledge Dr. Roberta Karant, my rock, who steadfastly declared that these concepts and the work they generated were important, and that sooner or later the world would recognize and begin employing them in psychotherapy, marriage, aging, parenting, education, staff development, and beyond.

My final acknowledgment goes to the dozens of volunteers and interns who have worked so hard to bring my ideas to life in our many programs. From among them I want to especially thank my editor Emily Wilson, who has patiently and intelligently guided the process of writing this book.

BREAKING THE "IMPOSSIBLE" CODE

0 01100101 01101100 01101111 01110110 01100101 01101100 01101111 01110110 01100101 011011

T he three happiest days of my life were when my daughter was born, when I married my wife, and when my granddaughter was born. The saddest days of my life have been when loved ones passed away, or when friends and family struggled through divorce and separation. Each event either brought more love into my life or left me with less. That's why I'm thrilled to offer you a book on my theory of love, a discovery I've made and have been successfully testing for decades—the theory that love is nourishment. I'm confident this book will help you safeguard the love you have and empower you to strengthen and deepen it, making it enduring and unshakable.

Over the last thirty years, I have helped countless people with their relationships. My work with individuals and couples has been very successful, and my presentations at major conferences are always well received. Despite this success, I resisted compiling my theories of love and human development into a book because I did not have hard scientific evidence to support my central thesis that love is vital nourishment.

In 2013, that changed. Dr. Barbara Fredrickson published her eight-year scientific study findings, showing that, just as I predicted years before, love is in fact nourishment. So, if you picked up this book because you want to improve your life and your relationships, give these concepts and exercises a try and see for yourself how transformative their practical applications are.

It is important to point out that your habits are deeply ingrained, and the actions and reactions that have been repeated over a lifetime will take time to unlearn. Ask yourself, "Is my happiness and that of those I love worth dedicating some time and effort?"

The ideas and exercises in this book will make an immediate difference, but the deeper, life-changing results that come from mastering a new approach to love and behavior take time. Patience and persistence are the keys to the kingdom.

A Recipe for Reading Together

Although I focus on committed romantic relationships, I designed this book to be read by couples, friends, siblings, and parents and children together as a relationship enrichment guide. For the sake of brevity, I will refer to each individual, regardless of the relationship's nature, as a *partner*.

Reading together ensures you'll be on the same page when working through the exercises. Using the exercises in this book can help relationships in the following ways:

- Learning what love is together will help each of you give it consistently.
- Understanding why being deprived of love causes pain will help you avoid behaving unlovingly.
- Rediscovering your lovable qualities and those of your partner will help you appreciate each other.
- Writing a relationship vision together gets any unspoken expectations and anxieties into the open. It will establish that

you are a team in full control over the direction and quality of your relationship.

- Practicing communication and listening exercises together will make you more compassionate when discussing difficult or emotionally charged topics.

Although you might be able to speed through the book in a few hours, I recommend you and (if applicable) your partner read no more than one chapter a day. Write down questions you might find answers to later in the book. Write down questions you might have for me, and attend our webinars for readers of this book. Slowing the reading process will give you time to use the exercises. By engaging with the material alongside your partner, you can develop trust that you are both committed to working on the relationship.

However, many of you may be reading this book on your own. I've found that in many relationships, one partner will be interested in personal enrichment workshops and books on relationships, whereas the other will decline invitations to participate. So, whoever has heard or read a tip will try and remember it and give a faithful account. Not surprisingly, most of what catches one partner's attention relates to something the other partner is doing wrong. Pretty soon, the other person picks up on this and starts to feel lectured to, and it all falls on exasperated ears. Defenses go up, loving communication ends, and an argument can break out—even if the other person realizes there is some truth to what is being shared. Why should they listen to criticism disguised as information? Even if the original intention to enrich the relationship is good, it is always better to model what you've learned instead of reporting it to your partner.

Here are some pointers on avoiding these thorny situations and inspiring your partner to read the book with you. After all, discovering new concepts and skills together creates a new bond and re-inforces the feeling that you're in it together. Here's an example of a dialogue you can have with your partner about reading this book:

> "There is something I would like for us to read together. Is this a good time to discuss it?"

If yes, proceed; if no, ask when a better time might be.

> "I love you and I know you love me. We have our moments, but we make an effort to be respectful, understanding, and supportive of one another. I have a feeling that you may not be interested in reading this book with me, but I would really appreciate it if you tried. I think it will be fun and that it will bring us even closer together. There are a few simple exercises that will be fun to do together. What do you say?"

If your partner refuses, resist getting angry and starting an argument. Say something like the following:

> "I am disappointed because I wanted to read it together, but I am not angry. Let me know if you change your mind."

If you find yourself reading this book alone, I challenge you to resist playing the role of teacher to your partner. Instead of trying to share your new knowledge, see if you can model what you're learning. Become more aware of your own unloving behaviors, learn to apologize more readily, and be more patient and understanding. In most cases, your new outlook and approach will positively influence your partner's behavior. In a few months, make the offer again.

When You're Feeling Alone and Unappreciated

By the time many partners pick up this book, they will have tried many ways to mend the relationship. Despite the effort, they feel unappreciated, taken for granted, or even unloved. They can't seem to get off square one.

Having succeeded in staying together is often a sign that there is love in the relationship. Even if it feels like the flame has gone out, it can be reignited. One of the keys to reigniting love is knowing that we need to give love as much as we need to get it. Just by beginning to give love and—this is important—showing appreciation, couples find they feel more hopeful. This is the start of the journey home.

Feeling unappreciated is painful. If this is an issue in your relationship, take two separate sheets of paper to make lists of things that you appreciate about each other and about the relationship. Is your partner honest, hardworking, dependable, funny, or smart? Does your relationship give you a feeling of security? Would your partner be there for you if there was an emergency? It doesn't matter how short the list is at first; post it on the refrigerator and add to it. As each list grows, so will the feeling that you both possess many qualities worth appreciating and you are being appreciated for them. Consider doing this and all the exercises in this book with your closest partners, not just your significant other. Mothers and daughters can benefit from this book and its exercises as much as couples can.

Once you and your partner have compiled a list of qualities you appreciate about each other, set aside ten uninterrupted minutes with your partner in a quiet setting each day for the next week. During that time, share your growing list with each other. At first, you may only think of big favors your partner has done for you that you appreciate, like that he or she drove you to the emergency room.

But as you continue this appreciation exercise throughout the week, you and your partner will find you both appreciate each other's little everyday acts and behaviors, like being on time, cleaning up after dinner, or texting or calling while away from each other. In time, we recognize how many things we take for granted and that we fixate on our partners' weaknesses. We can then see the degree to which that fixation undermines our relationships.

There is, of course, no silver bullet here. Once a couple experiencing difficulties has mastered this appreciation exercise, they must work on other exercises, like those in this book. Here's a good one to follow up the list of traits you appreciate about your partner. Create another list, this time of loving behaviors each person in the relationship performs. Add to it over time. When you catch each other behaving lovingly, draw a star on the list by the corresponding behavior. When you catch yourself behaving unlovingly, apologize and don't mark the list. As with the appreciation exercise, you will notice how we focus the negative aspects of our relationships and how easy it is for us to catch behaviors that are unloving or that we don't appreciate. If we want to retrain ourselves, we have to become conscious of this obsession with the negative and move toward catching behaviors that are loving and positive. This exercise brings out the best in both of you, the parts that you fell in love with.

The truth is that the love was never dead. It just needed to be nourished. I've compiled some of my theories on nourishing, loving relationships into nine points, which I collectively call the Nine Laws of Fulfilling Relationships. You may not understand them fully until you read through the book, but these principles are so valuable to a relationship that they warrant being printed out and posted near your bed to inspire you and your partner to grow closer together.

Enjoy the love.

NINE LAWS FOR FULFILLING RELATIONSHIPS

1. Love that has to be earned isn't love.
2. Become aware of your own and others' unloving, conditional behaviors as well as loving, unconditional behaviors.
3. Never reject others' loving energy. It hurts them.
4. Never allow others to behave unlovingly without consequence. It hurts you. Ask them to love you unconditionally.
5. Do not assume that there is any intentionality behind any act that hurts, disappoints, or angers you. Resist the temptation to blame others or assume their actions are designed to hurt you.
6. Assume all people, like you, are always doing the best they can.
7. Loving energy is real, nourishing, and visceral. It is like air, food, and water, and everyone needs to give and receive it in all our relationships, not just a few.
8. Loving energy has many names, like compassion, patience, affection, and thoughtfulness. It is not to be confused with automatic, physical, and sexual energy. Sweaty palms and fast heartbeats are biological signals for mating. I am talking about loving energy that nourishes us in a universal way.
9. The act of giving love must involve a conscious decision to be unconditionally loving even when you are upset with another person. You make the choice.

PART I

The best time to love with your whole heart is always now, in this moment, because no breath beyond the current is promised.

– FAWN WEAVER

LOVE UNRAVELED

Marriage or romantic commitment can be the ultimate showcase for the incredible power of unconditional love. Imagine describing your relationship in this way:

> We're two people who have, at the deepest level of our beings, a feeling of peace and serenity. We feel respected, accepted, appreciated, nurtured, and encouraged by each other and safe to say whatever we feel, and we enjoy communicating even about difficult topics where we don't see eye to eye. We are affectionate and considerate and have a tranquil family environment full of compassion and understanding.

This can be applied to any relationship, but it is possible only when partners are able to love each other unconditionally—and the result is incredibly joyful! I've seen it happen time and again with my clients. Reframing their ideas of what love is and why they need it completely turns around their approach to relationships.

We need to receive love consistently and unconditionally to experience true happiness, wholeness, and fulfilling relationships. When you're starved for love, your ability to make good decisions for yourself and your relationship is compromised.

Throughout this book, I'll be sharing stories of couples who came to me during rough patches in their relationships. Meet, for example, Doug and Jennifer, whose names have been changed for their privacy like all the names of couples in this book. And like all couples, they needed love, and they were dependent on love from each other. Over time, however, their blissful honeymoon period gave way to little arguments that blew out of proportion. She said he was controlling, he said she was critical, and neither felt loved by the other. Threats of leaving and divorce, far from convincing the other to admit fault, only raised tensions and made matters worse.

Like many others before them, Doug and Jennifer came to me partly to prove each other wrong, to convince each other that their problems were the other party's fault. Angry and hopeless, they thought that the only satisfaction left was to have a marriage counselor validate their own points of view.

I pointed out to Doug and Jennifer that they were in my office together, whereas many couples fought, separated, and divorced without ever making it to counseling. This meant that they both wanted somewhere deep down to make it work. Those parts of them still remembered how it felt to love and be loved in that relationship.

How frustrating would it be to send people to college without teaching them to read and write? It takes couples time to understand that problems in relationships are universal but can't be successfully solved without learning very specific tools and concepts. Likewise, it took Doug and Jennifer time to get past pointing fingers at each other. In the early days of their counseling, they would have five good days and then a blowup. They didn't appreciate the five good days, and the blowup was always the other person's fault. Sound familiar? As the focus changed from what wasn't working to what was, and they learned and practiced using the necessary tools, the blowups became less frequent. There was less blame thrown about and more personal responsibility taken. After a number of months of committed work, Doug and Jennifer realized that while they could not control the past, they were finally in control of their relationship's future.

The first order of business is learning how to become less dependent and more independent, and to learn how to love ourselves. That is the foundation for giving love and being able to do so unconditionally, and for creating close, loving relationships. This way, when relationship problems arise—such as arguments or unloving behaviors—we don't feel rejected and unloved. When our need for love is fully satisfied by loving ourselves, giving love to our partners, and receiving love from our partners, we feel a balanced sense of tranquility and contentment that simultaneously revitalizes us. We thrive and can become the individuals we want to be.

Love as Nourishment

Understanding the true nature of love is the first step to learning how to give and receive it freely and without condition. Love doesn't come wrapped in a cute little package we can buy for ourselves or hand over like a birthday gift. Have you ever asked yourself what love is? Perhaps not, since we all believe we know. We know what we experience; this powerful energy is felt in every cell of our bodies. We use words like *happiness* and *warmth* to convey the experience of love, as well as *pain, lethargy, heartache,* and *depression* when we are deprived of it. But these are descriptive terms about how love makes us feel—not what it actually is.

Like plants turning to face the sun, human beings are, in varying degrees, drawn to those who warm them with their love. The warmth that comes from most people some of the time and a few people all of the time nurtures and feeds us. When we receive the life-sustaining energies in air, food, and water, we thrive and feel energized, but when we are deprived of them, we experience physical pain and die. Similarly, when we receive loving energy, we also thrive and feel energized, but when we are deprived of love, we experience pain to the point that some people feel they want to die. Isn't *Romeo and Juliet*, a story of two people willing to die when love is lost, one of our favorite love stories? I've wondered, *Could it be that love also contains a life-sustaining energy? An energy that makes us feel like we're raring to go or, when we don't get it, like we can't get out of bed?* It would certainly explain why I was dizzy and bedridden for over a week after one instance of heartbreak, and why so many of us are endlessly searching for love. I studied our collective experience of love and became convinced that the desperation we feel when looking for love is like the distress of someone starving or dying of thirst.

I offer a new classification of love: an energy that nourishes and energizes us. It is an energy that we can get from another person, whether a partner or a stranger, and also give to ourselves. Love is an energy that behaves very much like the life-sustaining energies in air, food, and water.[1]

We have an expression in English and many other languages: three square meals a day. It pertains to all people needing and having the right to nourishment that allows their bodies and minds to function. When one is capable of providing for oneself, we call this self-sufficiency.

Loving energy is also necessary nourishment, so it's logical to say we should have three square meals of it every day. This doesn't mean

---

1. My hypothesis that loving energy is like air, food, and water is substantiated by the research of Barbara Fredrickson, PhD, at the University of North Carolina.

that we should only give and accept loving energy three times a day in large helpings. I use this expression here to say that loving energy, like food, is a daily necessity.

We've learned that loving behaviors give nourishing energy. When we are respectful, patient, or appreciative, loving energy is being generated by the giver and passed on to the receiver. In order to be truly self-sufficient, we must use the time for nourishing our bodies and brains to also nourish our hearts.

Let's see what this looks like in action.

Imagine sitting at your kitchen table or on a park bench, eating your lunch alone. To nourish your own heart with loving behavior, you pause for a couple of minutes to reflect on something like the following:

- I am a nice person who tries my best to be helpful. Even though I wish I exercised more, I like myself.
- I am honest and patient with others. Even though I wish I were more expressive, I like myself.
- I am handy around the house and my co-workers like me. Even though I am working on my temper, I like myself.

These thoughtful reminders ensure you care about and for yourself—not just the exterior, what the world sees, but also the inner, most vulnerable, most essential part. My clients who learn to incorporate these reminders into their daily lives say it is more nourishing than a hot bath by candlelight and more invigorating than a new eight-cylinder Camaro. Once you make a habit of reflecting like this, you will find yourself extending the same loving energy to others. You will remind them of their lovable qualities, knowing that people are not likely to feed themselves three nourishing meals of love a day.

Let's take a look at another set of properties life-sustaining energies have. Besides obtaining and ingesting air, food, and water, what else must we do? Would it be healthy if we only inhaled, ate, and drank?

Life-sustaining energies have a common quality: they are cyclical. That means for us to be healthy and have optimum energy, we must eat, drink, and expel. We must inhale and exhale. Have you ever experienced the pain of someone rejecting your love? We not only need to get love, we also need to give it.

When my precocious daughter was little, her grandfather used to kiss her almost nonstop anytime they were together. One day, after some time of putting up with his exuberance, she pulled away and told him, "Grandpa, I know you love me, but too much is too much." He was so heartbroken she'd rejected his affections that he didn't want to have dinner that night, and my mother had to explain to him that his granddaughter loved him but not the constant kissing. Eventually, he accepted her preference and he was able to both receive her love and give his love in a way that suited their needs.

Love has the same cyclical nature as food, water, and air—another indication that it is a life-sustaining energy. Realizing that we need to give love as much as we need to receive it is vital to our emotional and physical health. The difficulty is in keeping that loving energy flowing in a cyclical manner despite the urge at times to turn it off.

Can We Learn to Love Unconditionally?

Think of yourself for a moment as an electric generator that can be switched on or off. When we generate loving energy, the switch is activated by our conscious or subconscious thoughts. Most of us turn it on when we feel positively toward a person and turn it off when someone upsets us. Both our negative and positive reactions are mostly automatic, so the key is to learn to consciously turn the generator on and keep our hands off the switch even when we're upset.

We all need nourishing love, given and received unconditionally; and we need it from ourselves as much or more than we need it from others. In order for you to follow my line of thinking, I will give you my definitions of *unconditional love* and *conditional love* here.

- Unconditional love is loving energy consciously and consistently given and accepted, even under painful, upsetting, and disappointing circumstances.
- Conditional love is loving energy given and accepted only when you are pleased with someone you're in a relationship with, rather than under any and all circumstances.

During conflicts, loving energy is often either consciously or unconsciously withheld. When we're upset, we don't want others to try to be nice or in any way convince us to stop punishing them until we're good and ready. Even if our partners apologize, we often reject it because we don't believe they've served their sentence.

Even in the face of conflict, hurt, and anger, unconditional love requires us to receive and give love consistently. But this is very important: it does not require us to deny or disregard our hurt and anger or the behavior that caused it. Big difference! We can acknowledge hurt and confront unloving behavior while still loving the other person.

My father was a very affectionate, honest, hardworking man. He would come home and give me a big, sloppy kiss every night. But he also had a temper and would immediately raise his voice. Because he refused to listen to anybody and thought he was always right, I was afraid of telling him that his yelling upset me, lest he erupt into an outburst. His conditional behaviors made me completely turn my switch off. I neither felt affection for him nor wanted any from him, and the older I got, the more resentful I felt.

It wasn't until I got married and had a child of my own that I started to forgive him. I realized raising kids wasn't easy, and because he came from a home where only women raised children, he had even less insight into it than I did. My male friends aspired to be good parents and were much more involved in parenting than people like my father had been. Eventually, I also figured out how incredibly painful losing his parents and siblings in the war had been for him, and I started to appreciate that he was a human being who needed love. I recognized that he was doing his best, giving as much love as he could and still needing and deserving love from me, even though his behavior was hurtful and conditional.

In many ways I felt fortunate to have this insight, because without it I would have become increasingly alienated from him. This way, I was able to accept his affection and not take offense at his missteps. Not coincidently, the more I behaved with understanding and compassion toward him, the less he came to raise his voice and be argumentative.

Later in my practice, I shared my experience with many clients. I discovered that even clients who had lost their parents often had relationships with them that weren't buried. Once clients were able to view parents as a victims of their own families, as people who needed their love and were doing their best, their resentment softened, just like mine did. Often, without a word, without sitting down and having that heart-to-heart talk that many therapies engender— where adult children tell their parents how much childhood hurt, in a sense burying a knife deep into their parents' hearts—the relationship began to heal.

Of course, sitting down and telling parental figures that you know they loved you to the best of their abilities usually doesn't hurt, either.

It might surprise you to learn that your ability to be unconditional makes you very powerful. People think if they are unconditional, others will only take advantage of them. The reason we have this view is because seemingly nice people appear to put up with unloving behavior from others without any consequences. This book is not intended to be a psychological treatise, but we can safely say that, oftentimes, the reason people do not administer appropriate consequences for unloving behavior is because they fear loss. The more we feel dependent on someone else for love, the more likely we are going to look the other way when that someone behaves conditionally. This is very common in marriages and other close relationships. "If I complain too much or say that the next time we're going to time-out the relationship for a week, I'll be abandoned or neglected." Fear of some form of retaliation can stop people from administering consequences.

Unconditional love is not synonymous with weakness, dependency, or need, but rather comes from a cultivated inner strength—and therefore, it's not something that can be taken advantage of. As a matter of fact, someone who has cultivated the strength to stay loving under difficult circumstances also has the strength to say, "I love you, but this is not acceptable, and _____ will be the consequence if it doesn't stop." This unconditional behavior cultivates a great deal of respect, admiration, and even awe for you as other people realize they cannot affect you negatively. Remember, the greatest power human beings have is the ability to love, inspire, and motivate others.

Still, I've found in my years teaching unconditionality that many people struggle justifying the use of consequences with those who behave unlovingly toward them. How can we say we're being unconditional, they ask, if we impose consequences when someone hurts or disappoints us?

Let's examine what happens when we don't impose consequences.

1. The message often is that the hurtful behavior is acceptable. We can yell and scream, but it goes in one ear and out the other, and it causes people to double down on their hurtful behavior. Why should they make the effort to change their behavior if there are no consequences to staying the same?

2. When we tolerate hurtful behavior from someone, it creates resentment and distance in that relationship because we naturally protect ourselves. These negative feelings grow each time we tolerate an unloving act from others, and in time we start to dislike them and want to end those relationships.

3. When we don't impose consequences, it underscores the fact that we really don't love ourselves. With every unloving act we fail to challenge, we like ourselves less. We can begin to feel that we deserve people who mistreat us.

Let us also note that allowing people to behave unlovingly with us reinforces their propensity for exhibiting this behavior with others. This may lead them to have difficulty maintaining close, nourishing relationships. We're not doing them any favors by letting them mistreat us.

For relationships to work, we must love ourselves as well as others, and we must make abundantly clear what is acceptable and what is not. Consequences demonstrate to others that they will have to reconsider how much they value their relationship with you. If they value the relationship, they will make an effort to be more thoughtful and loving in their behavior.

Since there are no relationship schools to help us learn to love and be loved unconditionally, reading and sharing this book is a healthy start. Learning to love unconditionally takes dedication and a willingness to step outside your comfort zone. I promise you it will be worth it.

Take a few moments now to commit to loving yourself and your partner unconditionally. You will soon learn the tools that will help you to realize the incredible power of loving energy, so I encourage you and your partner to print and sign copies of the following personal pledges to demonstrate your dedication to unconditionally loving yourselves and each other.

PERSONAL
LOVE CONTRACT

0 01100101 01101100 01101111 01110110 01100101 01101100 01101111 01110110 01100101 011011

I, _____ , pledge to give myself and
my partner, _____ , unconditional love,
even during times of conflict and disagreement. Although I may be
angry, hurt, or upset, I pledge to express my feelings with love.

I know that an important part of loving myself is to only accept
loving behavior from others, including my partner.

Loving myself and others unconditionally makes me powerful, and
my loving behavior will help inspire others to grow and become
more unconditionally loving, themselves.

I understand that this is a process that will take time and that loving
unconditionally means being patient and persistent with myself and
others. I am committed to mastering the tools of awareness, vision,
and compassionate communication in order to love my partner unconditionally and make our relationship as strong, nurturing, and
fulfilling as it can be.

SIGNATURE _____

DATE _____

SELF-LOVE: WHY IT'S NOT SELFISH

W e all want loving relationships, but we can't love our partners until we love ourselves. This means knowing ourselves—embracing our strengths, weaknesses, and needs, and making sure those needs are being met. When we don't love ourselves, we have a tendency to accept unloving behavior from others. Subconsciously, we think this is all we deserve. People tend to treat us as we see ourselves. If you don't love yourself, guess how you will be treated!

When Julie and Martin came to work with me, they had already seen a number of therapists and a divorce attorney. There was very little respect and zero communication. They were exhausted by the impasse in the relationship. It was clear they were neither getting nor giving love to each other, nor did they love themselves very much.

I asked each of them to make a list of his or her own lovable qualities. Julie said she had none, but proceeded to write down three. Martin insisted he had none, and wrote none.

Their homework was to ask friends and relatives to add to their lists. The following week, Julie came in with tears in her eyes. She had felt all her life that her father did not love her. She sent him the list anyway and he sent it back with lots of lovable qualities she didn't think she had, but even more significantly, didn't think he saw in her.

As a result, her relationship with herself and others improved. She tried to have Martin add to her list, and she tried to add to his, but he would not share anything with her.

Martin, who refused to write any lovable qualities down, had nothing to approach friends and relatives with and refused to participate. Consequently, he was not able to get any positive feedback and was stuck disliking himself, which caused him to struggle giving and accepting Julie's love. Despite trying to be supportive and patient, not surprisingly, Julie eventually gave up trying to save their marriage.

You Deserve Self-Love, Not Self-Indulgence

In our culture, the phrase *love yourself* often conjures up an image of a selfish, self-centered, self-indulgent person. But selfish people only ask for help and are reluctant to give it, spend money on themselves but are stingy with others, and demand love without reciprocating. Loving yourself is different from that, but it isn't saying *yes* or constantly giving without ever asking anything of others. This supposedly unselfish attitude usually comes from feeling undeserving of love and support, and results in people feeling used and unappreciated. In truth, self-love has more to do with how we approach our relationship with ourselves than what we do or ask of others. It's true that some people can be whole unto themselves. They love and nourish themselves and do not need to ask for much from others. In many cases, however, this is an outward persona that has more to do with pride and a show of self-sufficiency than the way the person feels in reality.

Think of how lovingly you treat your best friend: with respect, appreciation, encouragement, patience, and compassion. The key is to apply that to yourself. Accept your weaknesses, appreciate your strengths, acknowledge that you are doing your best, and forgive yourself when you make mistakes. When we independently provide nourishing love to ourselves, we become our own best friends. As we can and want to bond with others, so we want and need to bond with ourselves.

Easier said than done? One of the first things you need to do to start on this path is to notice that there is a little voice in your head that is constantly talking. Raising and educating children is almost entirely focused on teaching new concepts and behaviors, which involves a constant stream of correction. Children start to internalize that critical voice and hear their own constant stream of self-correction. We become so used to it that we often don't even realize we're having a full-blown conversation with our inner selves. That little voice doesn't usually have many complimentary things to say to us, but it has plenty of critical, unkind things to say. If you believe what it says, it is difficult to like yourself, never mind love yourself.

Why would we treat ourselves this way? It's simple—there's no risk of losing a relationship with ourselves. We don't have to worry about getting the pink slip or being shown the door. No matter how poorly we treat ourselves, we're stuck with ourselves. This is the same reason that children and partners sometimes behave unlovingly. They're confident that they won't be fired.

As loud as the impatient, self-defeating voice in your brain can be and as soft as the encouraging signals are at first, the good news is *you* have the power to decide which to listen to. When the negative self-talk starts blaring, acknowledge the negative voice but choose to switch to a positive channel. Tell yourself that your endeavor will succeed, that your partner or friend will respond to your loving and persistent approach. Tell yourself, *I know I can do this if I am patient with myself.*

Make Unloving Behaviors a Thing of the Past

Think of the unloving behaviors you habitually inflict on yourself. Do you procrastinate when you know that it will hurt you? Are you impatient with yourself when learning something new? Do you dislike some physical feature, such as your hair or nose? Do you take your strengths for granted and harp on your weaknesses? Nothing hurts us more than not being accepted for who we are, and yet we do it to ourselves.

On your own sheet of paper, write the unloving behaviors you inflict on yourself, one for each day of the week. Now, write loving behaviors to replace them with. For example, on Monday, notice your strengths. On Tuesday, accept your weaknesses. On Wednesday, appreciate your physical features, and so on. Like this:

Sun	I don't get paid well	I'm updating my résumé
Mon	I don't feel smart	People laugh at my jokes
Tue	I'm always late	I will set more alarms
Wed	My clothes don't fit well	I love my hair texture

Revisit this exercise often. Whenever you notice yourself slipping into negative thoughts about your life or yourself, correct these thoughts by flipping them in a positive direction. This is a very important habit to cultivate because you first have to be aware of slipping, and then you have to gather your strength to pull yourself out of that negative space.

Making these little changes day in and day out will have a noticeable effect on your attitude, self-respect, and ability to nourish yourself with love. Even little changes have big effects over time, and you'll start to notice people reacting positively to your new outlook.

Sunday

Monday

Tuesday

Wednesday

Thursday

Friday

Saturday

Discover Your Lovable Qualities

Generally speaking, people have a very difficult time seeing themselves clearly. They struggle, in particular, with finding and remembering the good things about themselves. To help with this, I like to have my clients write a list of their lovable qualities. Again, if you don't think you're lovable, how will others?

This exercise is great to do with your partner because you can contribute to each other's list of lovable qualities. But self-love is so important that I insist you complete this exercise even if you're reading this book alone.

1. Print copies or draw the table on the next page. You get one and your partner gets one.
2. Think of three lovable qualities you possess and write those down under the *Me* heading.
3. Think about your partner's lovable qualities, and write three of them down under the second heading.
4. Think of your friends and family. What are three lovable qualities they might say you have? Write them down under the *Me II* heading. You should now have six different lovable qualities about yourself and three for your partner.
5. Once you've finished filling out your page, share what you wrote under the *My Partner* heading with your partner. Each of you should add these qualities to your own *Me* column. You each should now have nine lovable qualities under your *Me* heading.
6. Slowly read your nine lovable qualities to your partner. When you finish, see if you can remember each other's qualities.

Me

**My
Partner**

Me II

Continue adding to your list of lovable qualities by asking friends and loved ones what they love about you. We have this terrible habit of focusing on negative things, which sabotages relationships, sabotages life, and surely sabotages love. Acknowledging your negative inner voice but choosing to give thanks for all of your lovable qualities and those of your partner will start to change your perspective. Focusing on your lists of each other's positive qualities when you get upset or annoyed will eventually quiet the negative and reinforce the positive inner voice.

Self-Reflection: Making Time for You

Seeing and evaluating our own behaviors is often the last thing we want to do, and yet to love ourselves we have to become the foremost students of ourselves. We have to study and be honest about our behavior, taking responsibility for all of it—the good and the not so good.

Since it is difficult to see ourselves clearly in our totality, I suggest to my clients and students that they reach out to family, friends, neighbors, and coworkers. Start by writing down three of what you believe are your most obvious strengths and weaknesses. Afterward, ask two or three friends from your closest relationships what they think are your greatest strengths. To avoid rifts in those relationships, avoid asking your friends what your weaknesses are. Ask instead what aspects of your relationships with them they would like to improve upon, such as honesty, timeliness, or openness to new ideas. Avoid becoming angry or holding their opinions against them if they write something you don't like. Remember, where there is smoke, there is usually a fire, meaning if one person experiences a quality that does not flatter you, there is a chance that others may as well. Explanations for why we behave in certain automatic, unloving ways are okay, but they don't let us off the hook. We are still responsible for our behavior and the effect it has on others and ourselves. We may not like what we see, but loving ourselves means we can commit to learning new behaviors. Instead of using our energy to defend and explain our actions, we use that same energy to slowly, consciously substitute more loving behaviors toward others and ourselves.

A large part of this work includes understanding yourself, accepting yourself, believing in yourself, and forgiving yourself. This is extremely important, as loving yourself is the necessary foundation enabling you to persist toward your relationship objectives even when there are setbacks. If we don't love ourselves, we sabotage our relationships. We become impatient and blame others and ourselves during frustrating circumstances. Becoming aware of our weaknesses is something we usually shy away from, since we are often at a loss for how to manage them. But without acknowledging our weaknesses, we can't love ourselves fully, because in a sense, we're denying a part of who we are. Get to know your weaknesses the same way you get to know your strengths—by looking inside yourself and by asking loved ones—and remember that accepting your weaknesses is a sign of strength and a critical part of your personal growth.

The website JustSayYesToLove.com was originally conceptualized for singles to enrich their understanding of themselves and what constitutes the right relationship fit. In order to find the right person, you both have to be on a path to loving yourselves and others unconditionally, with the awareness, vision, and communication skills required to create and maintain a great relationship. As of September 2015, access is still free and people can use the information and questionnaires to enrich their understanding of themselves and what constitutes a potentially good fit. It is also a great tool for people in meaningful relationships. To receive the access code that will allow you to register for free, email love@thdc.org.

THE TRANSFORMATION OF RELATIONSHIPS

0 01100101 01101100 01101111 01110110 01100101 01101100 01101111 01110110 01100101 011011

The marriage or committed relationship is unique, containing an overwhelming amount of shared experience. Even if you are an only child, like I am, you are not likely to share as much of your daily life with a parent as you are with your partner. Marriage by nature involves constant discovery, some good and some bad, all of which requires continual adjustment. Each of us is in an ongoing growth cycle intellectually and emotionally, and the result is that the person you date is different than the person you marry, and the person you are on your wedding day is very different than the person you will be five, ten, or twenty-five years later. Your needs and expectations change through the years, and the person who's meant to fulfill them changes, too.

Decades ago, there were many external forces keeping marriages intact, including economic, social, and religious pressures. This has changed for many cultures, and in the stead of external forces that keep marriages together, today we get so-called advice from friends and the media. The messages from these sources often urge people who are not happy in their marriages to separate and find happiness elsewhere rather than inspiring the couple to seek solutions. They tell us that it's okay to take the easy way out, walk away, and not put the work in. They feed a fantasy that we're better than what we've got, that we deserve more. They tell us, "You could meet someone new tomorrow. John doesn't know how lucky he is. He'll be sorry when you walk out and will be begging you to come home."

Don't Be Fooled by Their Smiles

We know the difference between love and sweaty palms, but what about the difference between a loving relationship and a destructive one? Can we recognize the difference between a destructive relationship worth saving from one that isn't? It's difficult enough to navigate a relationship that's lost its spark, but trying to do so to a chorus of so-called friends singing their ideas of what love is or what you deserve can be confusing and downright unhelpful.

Figuring out whether a relationship is worth working on is not as complicated as it might seem. First, ask why your partner is in the relationship and what he or she wants out of it. This is a question you must answer, too. Asking this kind of question draws attention to the fact that there are issues worth examining regarding the quality of the relationship. Once you have both shared your answers, decide where you want to start mending. Does your partner's impatience upset you? Does your partner feel belittled by your criticism? Does one of you want to spend more time together? Each partner must begin mending the relationship with something doable that will let the other person know that both parties are invested in the relationship.

Do your part and observe your partner's behavior. If your partner appears to be putting forth effort, acknowledge it, vocally appreciate it, and give encouragement. If your partner does not seem to be trying, bring it up gently. Say, "I know the relationship is important to you, but it doesn't seem like you are trying. I still feel sad because you are impatient and loud with me."

When people insist they want the relationship but refuse to change their hurtful behavior, they need help, and that's okay. Addictions are another sign that one or both partners have a serious need for professional counseling. The major problem with addiction is how difficult it is for someone to admit he or she is addicted to alcohol, exercise, shopping, pornography, work, hoarding, or other behaviors.

If you decide that your relationship needs professional help, suggest to your partner, "I believe it when you say the relationship is important to you, but you don't seem to be able to control yourself. How do you feel about seeing a therapist?" It is possible your partner will resist, so offer to see the therapist together. In addition to helping your partner's progress, a therapist may be able to point out ways that *you* can be more loving in the relationship that you might never have thought of otherwise.

If even with time and patience your partner's hurtful behavior does not change, say, "If you want to continue in the relationship, you will seek help. I will come with you, but we need a professional's involvement." If this sounds like an ultimatum, that's because it is.

If either partner in a relationship doesn't want to change or seems incapable of changing the hurtful behavior in question, the relationship is destructive. Physical abuse is a clear sign of a destructive relationship, and the receiving party must seek outside help. Verbal abuse is trickier to pinpoint and we often discount its terrible effects, but it is no less a red flag, and it needs attention from a professional.

As in these cases, some relationships do need walking away from. But most of the time, the unhappiness in a relationship is a multi-faceted thing that doesn't involve physical or verbal abuse, and it can still be easily pointed to as so-called evidence that we deserve better. Our propensity for comparing ourselves to our peers fosters couple jealousy that can poison redeemable relationships.

We see that some people are seemingly perfectly happy in their relationships (which is often more public display than reality) and we feel that something must be wrong with our relationship or partner. Toxic thoughts creep in when we're around other couples, like "Susan doesn't appreciate me. She's constantly nagging me—not like Mike's wife, always bragging about how he fixed the car or put up the backyard fence." The effect is emotional exhaustion that stops people from trying their best to make the relationship work. Don't be sucked in, and don't compare your relationship to what others advertise for public consumption. Just focus on finding the answers that will make *your* relationship better.

According to my Continuum Theory© of Human Development, there are four basic parts to an unconditionally loving relationship.

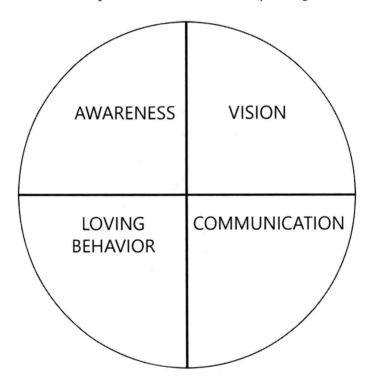

FIGURE 1   The four tools for an unconditionally loving relationship.

It's very likely that the trouble spots in your relationship land in one (or more) of the four areas of our model. This leads to what we call the Vicious Cycle you see below.

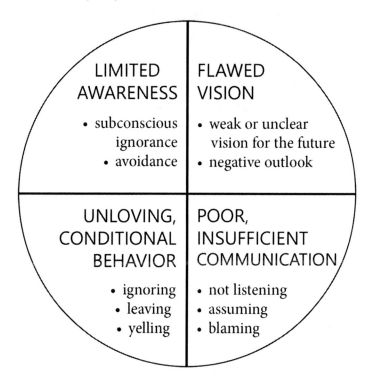

FIGURE 2   Where are your relationship trouble spots?

We'll discuss the four key aspects of an unconditionally loving relationship later. For now, start getting out of the habit of comparing relationships and finding flaws in yours. Take the time now to make a list of positive qualities about your partner and the relationship. Is there honesty? Dedication? Kindness? Willingness to share chores? Respect? Mutual interests or values?

Be sure that your partner makes a list, too. Use this opportunity to grow closer together by completing this exercise at the same time, like a project or a date.

Once you and your partner make these lists, you'll probably find that there are a lot more positive than negative aspects to the relationship. Armed with that knowledge, it becomes much easier to pinpoint the sore spots and work on them with an upbeat mindset. For those who find that the negatives outweigh the positives on paper, take a moment to let the following sink in: you and your partner have a long journey ahead if you want to make the relationship work. You and your partner will need professional help. And that's okay. What counts is that you recognize making changes and moving forward is necessary, and this book can help you.

Tell your partner something you appreciate about him or her. In a journal, write about your favorite memory with your partner, or about something you're looking forward to experiencing together in the future. Most importantly, try to become more aware of when you compare your relationship and your partner to others so you can override that negative pattern with positive, affirming thoughts like this one: "We're trying our best and are committed to enriching our relationship with these new tools."

The Tyranny of Expectations

People get married for lots of different reasons: because their parents expect it; because their religion, culture, or society has taught them it's part of adult life; because it makes sense for financial or legal reasons; or because they're in love and want to build a life together by taking another step in their committed relationship. The underlying similarity is that they all believe that marriage will improve their lives and bring them happiness. People enter marriage with the highest hopes and best of intentions, but it is often these lofty expectations of effortless happiness that undermine growth in a relationship and the hard work required to achieve it. Even twenty- or thirty-year-olds are relatively young and inexperienced when it comes to the emotional maturity that marriage and relationships require.

The traditional marriage vows don't contain the unconditionally loving component we need so much. *For better or worse, through sickness and health, till death do us part*—this phrase asks couples to stick together through the worst circumstances life can throw at them. It doesn't say anything about promising to love one another unconditionally throughout those circumstances. The reason we all declare these vows is because we all assume that unconditional love, the vital component to a loving relationship, comes bundled with this package. Most people believe that marrying someone who is caring and fun during the dating and engagement period, someone they love and feel loved by, means that the sense of peace, acceptance, and love they feel will last. We are not only full of hope that these wonderful feelings and behaviors will last a lifetime, we are *convinced* that they will.

Did You Skip Relationship School?

It's not that we're naïve or deluded. We know relationships take work. When you sit down with people and have a serious conversation about relationships, most couples will tell you that relationships aren't easy. They've seen their parents or friends struggle, and we're all familiar with the gloomy divorce statistics. In spite of the ability to intellectually recognize the challenges and realities of a lifelong commitment, another part of us is really in control, and that is the heart. The heart listens to logic and says, "Yes, but it will be different for us. We'll be one of the couples that makes it." Love is optimistic, and couples think that they can avoid the mistakes they made in their past relationships and prevent creating the same dysfunctions that their parents and relatives may have modeled for them.

As a therapist, I was curious to know what people really expected out of their marriages, why they decided to take the plunge knowing the statistics. My organization, The Human Development Company, interviewed hundreds of married, divorced, and engaged couples participating in our study. Here are the top expectations and reasons people gave for getting married:

1. Companionship
2. Children
3. Create a home
4. Security—both financial and emotional
5. To feel culturally normal
6. Available sex
7. Have someone to grow old with

As it turns out, many couples do in fact get all of these benefits and more in a committed relationship. They can have children if they choose, have a companion and consistent sex partner, plan for a home and retirement, and feel secure and normal in their chosen culture. In a marriage or committed relationship, people get what they expect and what they think they want, but half of them still get divorced.

So, what's missing? There has to be something else people yearn for on a deeper level, something they only become aware of when they start to feel restless or unhappy. It's only when they think about what went wrong that they realize something was missing. That something is unconditional love.

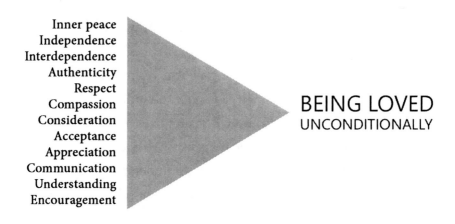

Inner peace
Independence
Interdependence
Authenticity
Respect
Compassion
Consideration
Acceptance
Appreciation
Communication
Understanding
Encouragement

BEING LOVED
UNCONDITIONALLY

FIGURE 3   Being loved unconditionally

Everyone I've worked with lets out a big sigh after seeing that list. We all yearn for these things, yet we cannot attain them unless we give and receive love unconditionally. This is what the fragile, hurting, childlike being inside all of us is calling out for: unconditional love we believe will heal our pain, fears, loneliness, or insecurity.

People want to believe that the close, loving bond of a new relationship will heal or mask their past hurt and prevent future pain. For many, the honeymoon period is euphoria not unlike that of a starving individual who finally finds a consistent source of delicious food. Why shouldn't this feeling of being consistently loved persist as long as we're with this wonderful person?

The problem is that there's no such thing as relationship school where we learn how to be loving in relationships. We have never been taught how to unconditionally love another person—especially when problems arise, which they inevitably do. When they do, we feel that the person we've chosen to trust with our hearts, the one who used to be so unconditionally loving with us, doesn't love us anymore.

Whether intentional or not, the result of that feeling is the same. The illusion is shattered, and we're left facing our fears and pain alone again. We're disillusioned, frustrated, and anxious.

Since we usually aren't able to pinpoint the sources of our pain (or acknowledge that we are in pain), a sense of confusion lingers and grows more frustrating with time. It makes us irritable and discontent. This spills over into our relationships. We expect our partners to read our minds when we ourselves don't understand the source of our own dissatisfaction or how to heal our wounds. In the next chapter, you will begin to acquire tools to effectively change all of that.

PART II

Success in marriage does not come merely through finding the right mate, but through being the right mate.

− BARNETT BRICKNER

AWARENESS: AWAKENING TO LOVE

0 01100101 01101100 01101111 01110110 01100101 01101100 01101111 01110110 01100101 011011

Even happy, fulfilling, respectful relationships go through rough spots. We all need the essential tools to help us love one another unconditionally: awareness, vision, and communication. Together, these create a feedback loop that, with unconditionally loving behavior, enables us to love and feel loved unconditionally.

In four chapters, we'll focus on developing these tools and applying them so that you can give and receive unconditional love in your relationships. It's important to remember that these tools are designed to be used holistically and sequentially—effective communication is impossible without a clear vision, just as creating a functional vision is impossible without deeper awareness. Because these skills are cumulative, it's important to read the chapters and exercises in order instead of bouncing around. Communicating can be disastrous without first having a thoughtful vision to guide what we want to achieve through our communication.

Here's an opportunity for you to see the stories of other couples learning to love unconditionally. As you read their stories of how they acquired and developed their relationship tools, spend a few moments thinking about how you would act in their situations. When you finish reading the book, I encourage you to go back and see how your answers have changed.

Francine and Larry

Francine and Larry were happily married for over ten years. But Francine became unhappy about getting older and became quiet, interacting as little as possible with Larry. Take a few moments and imagine yourself in their situation.

What do you think Francine was thinking and feeling?

What do you think Larry was thinking and feeling?

Without a vision for the relationship or an understanding of the necessity and power of communication or unconditional love, Francine and Larry drifted apart. She was busy with the children, and he was deeply involved with his business. When they came to me, they were very sad and convinced that they no longer loved each other.

What would you do if you were Francine?

What would you do if you were Larry?

_____

_____

Awareness: The Foundation of Conscious Behavior

Awareness, specifically of our feelings and thoughts, is like a muscle that needs development. To differentiate it from awareness of the world around us, we call it inner awareness.

Centuries ago, some members of the Chinese upper class bound girls' feet to keep them small. This permanently damaged the girls' muscles and bones. As adults, these women could barely walk; they certainly couldn't run, dance, or perform athletics. Inner awareness can similarly be affected when we are children. We are bound up by criticism, conditional love, impatience, or a lack of acceptance—even by well-meaning parents who simply don't realize they're behaving conditionally and don't know how to nurture a child's awareness.

Most psychotherapists, including Gestalt therapists, try to help people become more aware of their feelings and thoughts because it is the foundation for interacting with people. A developed inner awareness pays attention to your emotional inner state, and it tells you when things don't feel right in a relationship. Your awareness also establishes two important parameters, just like your GPS does: where you are and where you want to be. Without awareness of your current situation and how you feel about it, you can't begin to consider where you're going or how to get there.

It's equally important to become aware of your own actions and their effect on other people. For instance, you may not even realize you are doing something unloving while you are doing it. One indicator that can help you become more aware of these actions is noticing other people's reaction to your behavior. Do they fall silent or snap? Mutter defensively? Tear up and leave the room? Not call or answer the phone for days or weeks? To have close relationships, we first have to commit to paying close attention to the way others react to our behavior and take it to heart.

Instead, our tendency is to defend our own behavior or call someone "too sensitive." As you develop your awareness, you will have the ability to evaluate your own motives and behaviors and consider the effect they may have on the other person before you speak or act. How often has something slipped out of your mouth and you immediately regretted or questioned it? It happens to me, too, but now I can notice, be understanding of the other person's reaction, and say, "I'm sorry, that came out wrong."

Building Awareness

Even in close relationships, we may take things for granted or not notice bad habits are developing. We lose awareness of the details and might not realize that we don't fully understand the basics.

For example, how do you define love? What is your partner's definition of love? I'll bet you haven't really discussed it—perhaps you never sat down to really think about it yourself—but it is one of the main causes of friction. We not only expect our partners to automatically know our definitions of love and the expectations that follow, we actually expect them to have the very same definition and expectations as ours. What a recipe for discord and disaster!

Let's explore these issues and bring some clarity to what your definitions of love are and how they color your expectations. Here are

examples of some of my clients' expectations based on their definitions of love.

Client 1

- Remembering birthdays
- Keeping holidays
- Buying gifts
- Being courteous
- Going on vacations
- Calling regularly
- Controlling one's temper
- Willingness to help

Client 2

- Being respectful, affectionate, and appreciative
- Being thoughtful, kind,
  and considerate
- Being patient, accepting,
  and understanding
- Communicating

Client 3

- Sharing responsibilities
- Spending quality time
  with each other and the
  children
- Being authentic
- Being intimate
- Forgetting little upsets
- Forgiving big upsets
- Accepting each other's
  family

Each person had a very different understanding of love. Imagine
the repercussions of having such disparities with your partner and
not knowing it! One couple I worked with constantly butted heads
because his idea of love was "accept my family and spend lots of time
with them," but she felt very uncomfortable around his family. And

her idea of love was "buy me expensive birthday gifts and take me on nice vacations," but he felt uncomfortable spending money. So, they both felt unloved! They needed to create a shared vision—with compromises they committed to—in order to start communicating better about these thorny issues and to feel loved. Becoming aware of your expectations and those of your partner is a critical step in making each other feel loved and cherished. Take some time to write your definitions of love. This will grow your awareness in preparation for your shared vision.

Once you and your partner write your definitions, share them slowly and thoughtfully. Let your partner's ideas of love sink in, because without understanding them, you will likely fall short of making your partner feel loved. You may be surprised by your partner's definition of love. It's important that you discuss each other's reactions (of surprise, disappointment, or joy, for example) and commit to understanding and accepting them rather than criticizing and rejecting them.

VISION: THE LOVE MAP

Francine and Larry each spent some time developing awareness. Francine began by considering what she was already aware of: she felt unhappy about getting older and uncomfortable in her own skin—something she considered a personal problem she thought she needed to deal with on her own. As she deepened and expanded her awareness, she realized that her sense of needing to deal with the problem on her own—and not communicating that to Larry—made him feel unloved. She began to realize something universal to all relationships: her problem was not hers alone, but also a problem in the relationship. What she initially thought was a personal problem was affecting her husband and their relationship without her realizing it.

Meanwhile, Larry began by focusing on what he was currently aware of: his sadness that Francine was pulling away from him, his hurt that she wasn't showing him affection, and his frustration that she would not communicate with him about it. As he deepened his awareness, he realized that his frustration was slowly turning into resentment, which was getting in the way of them reconnecting and working through the problem together.

Francine and Larry worked to enhance their shared awareness and found they each had an underlying sense of hopelessness that was preventing them from having a breakthrough. With all of this newfound awareness, they were able to create an effective vision to actively mend and strengthen their bond.

No Vision, No Change

Have you ever run out of a few essential items, grabbed your car keys, and gone to the supermarket? I have, and I came home with three things I didn't need and managed to forget the very items I went out to buy in the first place. Frustrated, I had to turn around and go back. When some people need to replenish their cupboards, they do it thoughtfully. They take inventory, look at each shelf, make lists, and have a much better chance of coming home with all the right items than the person who did a quick mental inventory.

When most of us think of *vision*, grand accomplishments come to mind, like Martin Luther King Jr.'s vision of racial equality or Kennedy's vision of landing on the moon. Vision implies that we see our goal very clearly, almost to the point of being able to hold it in our hands—like an architect's draft or a business plan. Visions require that we take time to think about what we want to create, write it down in detail, and persist until it's achieved.

Have you ever written a vision for any of your relationships? Most people think that sounds funny, and yet that is exactly what is missing from many struggling or unsatisfying relationships. The most pervasive reason relationships can become aimless, disappointing, and unfulfilling is because they lack a conscious vision to direct each partner's actions and choices.

Consider how you approach each day. Do you jump out of bed with a tune on your lips or do you have to drag yourself out from under the covers? If it's the latter, your enthusiasm is likely near zero and you are anticipating a day full of headaches, lingering problems, or troublesome people. You need gallons of coffee just to autopilot through your day. Perhaps you'll simply choose to avoid the issues, leaving them to fester and stink up the next day.

The Choice is Yours

All of this *Sturm und Drang*, the drama in relationships and life, is primarily because of a lack of thoughtful vision. Nobody's life is perfect, but what if your vision for each day was to do your best to be productive, have fun, address problems head-on, and trust that everything will work out? What if you had a similar vision for your relationship? "I love my wife, and she loves me. I appreciate her strengths and accept her flaws, just as she appreciates and accepts mine. I feel at peace because we know how to listen and talk to each other about anything that may come up." Doesn't that sound great?

Some people might think this sounds ridiculously simple: create a vision and problems disappear. No, the problems don't disappear, but your approach to handling them changes. When your approach changes, you have a calm confidence that affects others, encourages compromise, and leaves a lot of energy for constructive creativity and motivation to persist until a problem is resolved.

Have you ever seen the film *Groundhog Day*? It's about how our vision for life, starting with our vision for each day, affects our experience. Bill Murray's character finds himself reliving the same day—February 2—over and over again. It feels like a curse. At first he becomes incredibly frustrated because he's stuck in a loop where nothing he does matters. He slips into bitterness and depression, and thinks up a different way of ending his life each day, only to wake up the next morning having to start all over again.

Then, his vision changes. He decides he can use the endless amount of time he has to learn skills and do good in the community, like rescuing a boy who falls out of a tree, taking piano lessons, saving a man from choking on his dinner, and learning French. This leads him to build relationships with people. By the end of the film, he has enriched his life, fallen in love, and broken the Groundhog Day curse.

The key to his success was transforming his vision for each day from cursing it to realizing that great possibilities exist. Enjoying life starts with having loving relationships, and those require thoughtful visions.

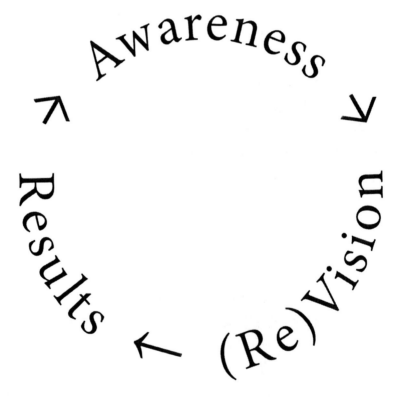

FIGURE 4   In a vision feedback loop, you build a vision to change your mindset and behavior based on your awareness. With the results from your changed behavior, you use your awareness to continually improve your vision.

A thoughtful plan for growth, healing, and loving relationships is worth taking time to create. Remember that although a written vision is necessary for moving forward with resolve, it is a living plan that is subject to change and growth. It becomes a feedback loop.

As we begin to work with our vision, we encounter setbacks, learn more about ourselves, and see the effects our new behaviors have on others. This creates a greater awareness of our relationships and our own needs, which we can then use to revise and improve our visions. The cycle continues as our visions continually evolve and help us reach our true goals.

By using the list on page 49, you can get an ideal relationship vision. Work alongside your partner if you're reading together. (But be sure to do this exercise even if you're reading by yourself! Everyone needs a vision.)

Prioritize what you consider to be the most important qualities in your relationship to the least important. If going in numerical order overwhelms you, try agreeing with your partner on a system, like writing *A* for the nine most important qualities, *B* for nine important qualities, and *C* for the nine less important qualities in your ideal relationship. These qualities are all important, of course, but prioritizing allows us to focus on one thing at a time rather than be overwhelmed with an enormous emotional to-do list.

Once you're done filling out and talking about your relationship blueprints, write down your partner's top nine important qualities on the back of your sheet. This will ensure there's clear communication between you and your partner.

Next, think back to Francine and Larry. They had only one vision directing their behavior: *for better or worse, in sickness and health, till death do us part.* That vision kept them together but unfortunately did not give them ways to turn their situation around. Like almost every other couple on Earth, they never created a written vision for their relationship. Visions drive behaviors and choices, and without having a vision they just kept repeating the same behaviors over and over. Many partners feel trapped in the relationship when actually they are trapped in their own limiting vision and behaviors.

One of the first things we do when couples seek counseling is have them write a vision. It includes practically everything they can think of wanting from their partners and the relationships.

Knowing now the importance of vision in relationships, what other elements do you think Francine and Larry should include in their vision? What would you do?

State of Our Relationship

- ☐ My relationship is nurturing, joyful, and enduring.
- ☐ My relationship is effortless.
- ☐ My relationship is easy to understand.
- ☐ My relationship is respectful.
- ☐ My relationship is supportive.
- ☐ My relationship is committed.
- ☐ My relationship has great communication.
- ☐ My relationship is peaceful.
- ☐ My relationship is like teamwork.
- ☐ My relationship is always growing and maturing.
- ☐ My relationship is unconditionally loving.
- ☐ My relationship is sexually satisfying.
- ☐ My relationship is built on trust.
- ☐ My relationship is an equal partnership.
- ☐ My relationship is physically tender and affectionate.
- ☐ In my relationship, we agree on spending.
- ☐ My relationship is encouraging.
- ☐ My relationship is characterized by compromising.
- ☐ My relationship is based on forgiving.
- ☐ In my relationship, each of us has a good sense of self.
- ☐ My relationship is based on fairness.
- ☐ My relationship is based on honesty.
- ☐ In my relationship, we are faithful to communicated boundaries.
- ☐ My relationship is based on mutual appreciation.
- ☐ My relationship is based on a deep understanding each other.
- ☐ In my relationship, we agree on whether to have and how to raise children.
- ☐ In my relationship we are democratic.

Crafting a Dynamic Vision

How do we create a vision that encompasses the constant changes and fluctuations of a relationship?

For starters, we need to focus on the things that will never change. Both you and your partner will always require the other to be honest and behave lovingly and unconditionally.

Secondly, both of you will always need to feel heard. Your vision must therefore reflect that, throughout the relationship, you will both cultivate awareness, loving behaviors, and communication skills, which together will help you work through issues and disagreements that may arise. When communication is effective and you're living with someone who loves you unconditionally, there is nowhere else you want to be. You will handle major life changes or challenges so a solution that keeps the relationship strong will present itself.

Here are three lists to get you started. After filling them out, use the prompts that follow to write your vision of the kind of partner you want to be in the kind of relationship you want to have. Invest time and thought into your vision and revisit it. Then, sit down with your partner to create a shared vision for your relationship. Include what each of you need from each other, even if it is not available yet.

Visions are living documents. Keep talking about your shared relationship vision and revise it, particularly during milestone moments. Remember the vision feedback loop: your vision must reflect your awareness, so small revisions will occur almost constantly. Make a concerted effort to make big revisions to your personal joint visions for big changes. Update your vision if, for example, you have children, buy a house, relocate, change jobs or take on different career roles, become empty nesters, or retire. Don't let it collect dust; like any living thing, your relationship vision needs attention and care.

Relationship Blueprint

- ☐ I want our relationship to be enduring.
- ☐ I want our relationship to be effortless.
- ☐ I want our relationship to be respectful.
- ☐ I want our relationship to be supportive.
- ☐ I want our relationship to be intimate.
- ☐ I want our relationship to be peaceful.
- ☐ I want our relationship to be appreciative.
- ☐ I want our relationship to be patient.
- ☐ I want our relationship to be nurturing.
- ☐ I want our relationship to be encouraging.
- ☐ I want our relationship to be unconditionally loving.
- ☐ I want our relationship to be sexually satisfying.
- ☐ I want our relationship to be physically tender and affectionate.
- ☐ I want our relationship to be positive and joyful.
- ☐ I want our relationship to be healed or healing.
- ☐ I want our relationship to be always growing and maturing.
- ☐ I want us to be equal partners in our relationship.
- ☐ I want our relationship to be based on honesty and trust.
- ☐ I want our relationship to be based on fairness.
- ☐ I want our relationship to be based on great communication.
- ☐ I want our relationship to be based on commitment.
- ☐ I want our relationship to be based on mutual appreciation.
- ☐ I want our relationship to be based on compromises.
- ☐ I want our relationship to be based on forgiving.
- ☐ I want our relationship to be based on learning and growing.
- ☐ I want our relationship to be accepting and understanding.
- ☐ I want our relationship to be based on faithfulness to communicated boundaries.

I Want to Be . . .

☐ accepting   ☐ spiritual   ☐ aware

☐ unselfish   ☐ vulnerable   ☐ positive

☐ honest   ☐ interested   ☐ grounded

☐ supportive   ☐ interesting   ☐ content

☐ forgiving   ☐ nurturing   ☐ patient

☐ loving   ☐ communicative   ☐ encouraging

☐ confident   ☐ easy-going   ☐ appreciative

☐ fun   ☐ funny   ☐ healed or healing

☐ imaginative   ☐ independent   ☐ respectful

☐ practical   ☐ secure   ☐ affectionate

☐ trusting   ☐ friendly (a friend ☐ emotionally

☐ trustworthy   ☐ joyful   available

I Want My Partner to Be . . .

☐ accepting   ☐ spiritual   ☐ aware

☐ unselfish   ☐ vulnerable   ☐ positive

☐ honest   ☐ interested   ☐ grounded

☐ supportive   ☐ interesting   ☐ content

☐ forgiving   ☐ nurturing   ☐ patient

☐ loving   ☐ communicative   ☐ encouraging

☐ confident   ☐ easy-going   ☐ appreciative

☐ fun   ☐ funny   ☐ healed or healing

☐ imaginative   ☐ independent   ☐ respectful

☐ practical   ☐ secure   ☐ affectionate

☐ trusting   ☐ a friend   ☐ emotionally

☐ trustworthy   ☐ joyful   available

Vision for Relationship

Take a few moments and create a vision for the kind of partner you want to be. What qualities, habits, and attitudes do you want to bring to your relationship?

_____

_____

_____

_____

_____

_____

_____

_____

_____

Vision for Relationship Needs

Take a few moments and think about what you need from your partner in order to feel unconditionally loved. What qualities, habits, or attitudes do you want your partner to bring to your relationship?

_____

_____

_____

_____

_____

_____

_____

_____

_____

Joint Vision for Relationship

Sit down together and devote some time to talking about how you each envision your relationship. What qualities, habits, and attitudes do you want to establish in order for your relationship to thrive and grow? Which of your habits do you want to keep or further develop? What issues do you want to address or improve? Make this vision as complete as possible, and remember to revisit and revise your vision periodically.

COMMUNICATION: LOVE'S TWO-WAY STREET

0 01100101 01101100 01101111 01110110 01100101 01101100 01101111 01110110 01100101 011011

Not surprisingly, Larry wanted more time with and affection and communication from his wife. The fact that Francine wouldn't tell him what was going on for her made him feel that Francine had stopped loving him, which she fervently denied. She actually thought everything was okay with the relationship and that *she* was the problem. She felt lost and confused and did not know where to turn for help. Larry felt disrespected and said that Francine's willingness to communicate with him would show respect and trust in him and their relationship. They created a very simple vision where the priority was communication followed by affection.

What do you think about this vision? Would you have included other elements?

Is there a lingering issue in your relationship that could use a vision for communication to help resolve it?

....

....

....

....

Communication: the Lifeblood of Relationships

Relationships are not static entities. As much as you may think that things are pretty much the same as they were five, ten, or fifteen years ago, they aren't. Relationships either move in a positive direction or they deteriorate. Because change happens slowly, it's easy to believe that a relationship is okay, and partners can tolerate, get used to, or overlook negative changes. One day, a partner wakes up to find the other wants a divorce. This is one of the reasons why intentional, thoughtful communication is so important for healthy relationships.

When is the last time you and your partner had a "state of the union" discussion? Do you talk about issues as they arise or let them fester? I strongly encourage all my couples to ask one another these four questions on a regular, weekly basis:

- Are you happy with your life?
- Are you happy with our relationship?
- Are you happy with me?
- What can I do to help you to be happier?

Once you become acquainted with the tools in this book that will help you on your journey to loving unconditionally, add these questions to your state of the union discussion:

- Do you feel unconditionally loved by me?
- What words or actions help you to know I love you unconditionally?
- What words or actions suggest that there are conditions to my love?

Ultimately, some of the issues affecting relationships have little to do with the partner. Work stress, health problems, financial worries, and other external factors can affect personal stress and relationship health. How reassuring is it to know that you can create a life-support system in your partner, someone who is always there to encourage you and, more importantly, to just listen?

Get into the habit of having a weekly heart-to-heart to check in with each other and reconnect. I guarantee you will both look forward to it, because it will validate why you love each other. You know you're there to support each other not only in times of crisis but also through the myriad of daily struggles.

Another wonderful relationship habit to cultivate is making lists of things you are thankful for—in gratitude journals or on sticky notes you can leave on each other's pillows or desks. Being grateful takes the focus off of the things that aren't going well and reminds you how much more there is to be thankful for so you don't take them for granted. This new perspective also changes your mindset to help you use your energy constructively, rather than getting mired in negative thoughts that are draining the life out of you and your relationship. Unchecked, these negative thoughts snowball into tiffs and worse.

Couples will do almost anything to avoid fights and confrontations, especially when they're afraid of seeming petty or overly sensitive about their sore spots. We wonder, *Shouldn't it be obvious after all this time?* The problem is that no one is a mind reader, and your partner can't figure out what may be troubling you without your help. If you love your partner, isn't it easier to communicate what you want or don't want than to get angry, pout, or withdraw?

One of the most common complaints I've heard about communication is that people repeat themselves over and over about something that upset them and they just can't let it go. "How many times are you going to bring this up?" the other person responds. "You said it twenty times already. I got it, I got it."

No, you didn't.

The number one rule in communication is that when someone feels heard—really understood—the issue will be dropped. It becomes old news. If you find your partner harping on the same issue, you can be sure your partner has never felt truly heard. Sure, it went into your ear, but the other person's experience is that it went right out the other. You need to go into active listening mode and say, "It seems like you don't feel that I heard you the first time. I'm sorry—let me make sure I really pay attention this time." (We'll discuss active listening a little later.)

Very often people are puzzled by the idea of having to learn communication techniques. Doesn't everybody know how to communicate? That is certainly how Francine and Larry felt. But effective communication implies that when problems are discussed, it leads to an agreeable resolution and actually brings two people closer together. When Francine and Larry discussed problems, they usually ended up in an argument that made things worse. In a day or two things would blow over, but the relationship made no progress. Like many of us, they were hesitant to even start difficult conversations. "It's small stuff. There is no need to be petty," they would explain, but every time they did, a little more resentment piled up in the corners of their hearts.

If you and your partner were drifting apart, how would you begin the conversation to repair the relationship? How do you think that conversation should go?

Sticks and Stones May Break My Bones, but Words Will Surely Kill Me

Long after bruises and broken bones have healed, we remember someone's thoughtless or ill-advised comment. We must become more conscious and aware of how hurtful words and behaviors can be, and how those wounds may never completely heal.

Mirroring is a great communication tool. It focuses on intentional communication and active listening, and the reason it's effective is it makes our desire to understand others very clear to them. That is the unconditional part of the equation. Unconditional communication means putting aside your personal agenda and focusing all your energy on the relationship—making sure the other person feels that you really care about hearing what is being said.

Simply put, mirroring involves repeating word for word two to three sentences at a time that one person says to another. It involves a person who wants to communicate (the *sender*) and a person who will be listening and repeating (the *receiver*). Follow these steps:

1. Sit face-to-face in close proximity and determine who is the sender and who is the receiver. The sender asks, "Is this a good time to talk?"
2. If not, both agree on a later time. If it is a good time, the sender begins, "I know you love me and you know I love you." The sender adds a couple of positive adjectives that describe the receiver.
3. The sender begins a message with a couple of short sentences.
4. The receiver says, "What I'm hearing you say is . . ." and repeats the sender's sentences verbatim. When finished, the receiver asks, "Did I hear you correctly?"

5. The sender indicates *pass* or *no pass*. In instances of the latter, the sender repeats the sentences until the receiver gets a pass.

6. The receiver asks each time, "Is there anything more you would like to say about that?"

7. Continue until the communication is complete.

Take special note of the question the receiver needs to ask after repeating the communication and getting a pass. Ask, "Is there anything more you would like to say about that?" When doctors clean wounds, they don't just do half the job, leaving the area ripe for infection. Unfortunately, that is often what we do when communicating during conflicts. We don't want to hear it, so we try to interrupt or stop it. It winds up leaving a lot of dirt in the other person's wound, which will fester and infect the relationship over and over again.

Mirroring is not designed as conversation. It short-circuits our propensity for responding automatically and develops our ability to be thoughtful when communicating. Focusing on saying a few sentences at a time (so the receiver can hear and repeat what is said) forces the sender to slow down and actually think about what to say. This prevents the high-speed rattling we tend to do when upset.

The receiver, by having to concentrate and remember what is being said, is better able to shut down defensive inner dialogue, is less likely to interrupt or misinterpret what the sender is saying, and is able to stay present in the conversation. The sender, meanwhile, feels heard, feels safe, and feels that the receiver values the sender's perspective. Both partners are better able to remain calm and lower mounting defensiveness and escalating emotions. The message is communicated and understood more effectively.

Many people ask me how they apply mirroring in their relationships when they are the only ones who know about it and are practicing it. The good news is it only takes one person. If confronted or asked why you're repeating everything, you can explain, "I want to make sure that I hear everything you're saying. This helps me to respond more appropriately. I want you to know that you're important and what you're saying is important to me."

Effective communication depends on two crucial components: knowing how to constructively express your concerns instead of holding them in, and iterating your loving connection at the start of such communication. Expressing anger is healthy, but it can be a slippery slope if we don't know how to express our anger lovingly.

Here is a situation that shows you how a typical communication about hurt feelings can be delivered in a negative way and then a positive way. Imagine your partner saying this to you:

> You don't love me. You could have come with me to the ball game, but getting together with your silly girlfriends is more important to you than I am. You couldn't care less about me.

How would you react to hearing that? How would you feel? Defensive? Angry? Incredulous? This is conditional behavior and it does not communicate the truth. It only communicates what may feel like the truth in the heat of the moment. People hate to be misrepresented, and statements like this almost always lead to a defensive counterattack. Instead, imagine your partner expressing his or her feelings in the following way:

> I know you love me, but it didn't feel like it. It felt like your friends were more important to you than I am when you chose to be with them instead of coming to the game with me. It hurt and angered me.

Remember, acknowledging that your partner loves you first and then saying that you're hurt allows for the right emotional environment to discuss the issues and reach a positive resolution. Each time we resolve a relationship problem—however big or small—it adds positive momentum to our feedback loop.

Whenever my wife got upset, her way of expressing discontent was to give me the silent treatment. I tried to talk to her and resolve the problem, but what I didn't realize was that I kept coming to her with logical arguments to explain my side of things, not affection. It's common for some people to focus on winning an argument or justifying their positions, but this doesn't lead to a positive resolution.

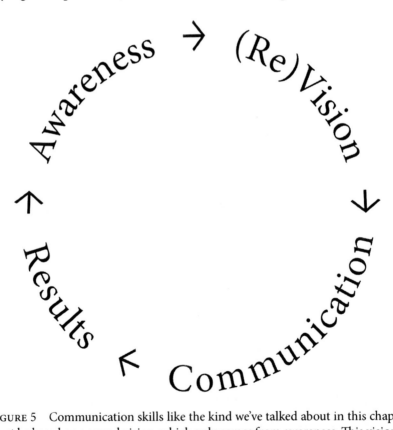

FIGURE 5 Communication skills like the kind we've talked about in this chapter must be based on a sound vision, which only comes from awareness. This vision is changed by the results of our successes (and failures) in communication.

It's important to express affection and reestablish the love present in the relationship first. We want compassionate communication to inspire the other person to seek growth.

The need for communication usually arises from being upset or witnessing a behavior you want someone to change. Much of our communication is about what we want without considering others' needs. They are expected to understand your feelings and adjust their behaviors to satisfy you. Communication is most effective, however, when its purpose is to support and inspire your partner in the relationship. We all find growth difficult and need our partners' patience and compassion—not to mention our partners' unconditional love—to accomplish it.

UNCONDITIONAL LOVE: IN OUR DNA

As you've learned, it's always best to start communication by reestablishing the emotional connection of the relationship. People are together because they love each other, but if they don't have the tools to deal with problems and disagreements, they get frustrated with the other person.

As we've discussed, ineffective communication can leave frustrations unchecked and fights unresolved, which can make partners feel unloved even if they *are* loved. The truth is simple and would sound something like this: "I am frustrated by my inability to effectively get across what is troubling me and by your inability to listen to me and help resolve my issue."

Francine and Larry said to each other, "I know you love me, and you know I love you," and it dissolved the fear of rejection. They realized they loved each other and could breathe again. They were able to listen to each other and work together to resolve the problem.

The rest was just mirroring. Francine explained to Larry that she felt older and insecure. She was afraid to say anything because she didn't want anyone to try talking her out of her feelings. She didn't realize how much it was hurting Larry. And he told her she was beautiful and desirable in his eyes. While it took her a little while to accept that as truth, the cycle of distancing stopped and healing began.

Is there a little issue in your own relationship that has lingered for too long? An issue that mirroring and saying "I know you love me and you know I love you" to each other might begin to resolve?

_____

_____

_____

_____

Loving Unconditionally

The dating and courtship process is full of unconditional behavior. When a relationship is new and fragile, partners tend to behave more lovingly—showing respect, appreciation, patience, and flexibility—than they do after a few years of being together. Since the relationship is unconditional in the beginning, both parties have every reason to believe it will continue being unconditional as time passes and the relationship moves forward. And who wants to think otherwise?

Think back to the first time you got sick while in the early stages of dating your partner. You canceled dinner plans because of your terrible cold, and instead of getting frustrated or angry, your partner rushed over with something warm to eat, cough syrup, and a stack of movies. He or she took care of you, not minding your contagious germs or that you were wrapped up in an unflattering bathrobe with used tissues falling out of your pockets. You and your partner were likely unconditional with each other.

But now that you've been together awhile, the moment you say, "I think I'm coming down with something," your partner takes five steps backward. Catching a cold means one of you sleeping on the couch to avoid catching the bug. Your partner might even say, "Ugh, why can't you throw your disgusting tissues in the trash? They're all over the house!"

This doesn't mean that your partner loves you any less now than before. In fact, your partner's love for you has likely grown and deepened as your relationship progressed. But once the relationship gets more secure and each of you feels more comfortable, automatic and conditional behaviors start to creep back in and replace the conscious, unconditional responses we were spoiled with at first and now rightly expect and deserve.

The Keys to Remain Loving during Conflict

Have you ever seen a reprimanded child cry and reach out to a parent? The instinct in human beings is always to keep the connection, to keep this loving energy flowing.

Children have love barometers that function perfectly, and they don't want that loving energy turned off. Unfortunately, many parents—not to mention siblings, friends, and schoolmates—often reject attempts at maintaining the flow of love. We learn that reaching out during quarrels or being a peacemaker is often unwanted, and as our instinct to stay connected erodes over time, we prioritize self-preservation. To avoid more hurt, adults cut our emotional losses and begin controlling the impulse to reach out and stay loving during painful moments.

It's easy to knock heads with someone who always wants to communicate when we need time to cool off. It's also easy to call others

out and claim to be more mature than they are because we are willing and able to address conflicts right away rather than stew like they
do. But neither of these are unconditionally loving behaviors, and
unconditional love is crucial in times of conflict.

Sit down with your partner (when you're not upset) and acknowledge the differences in the way you two communicate during conflict. Talk about the importance of staying connected and make
an agreement to be physically connected when communicating by
holding hands, especially when upset. Rather than assuming one
person's way of handling conflict is better, ask each other questions
like the following:

- How do you feel when we talk about conflict?
- Do you need time to cool down?
- Do you need space to think?
- Do you need to hold hands or feel affection?
- Do you shut down when there's yelling?
- Do each of you know and understand the other's way of com-
  municating?
- Can you accept each other's modus operandi while commit-
  ting to move toward the other's way?

Remembering the child within all of us, the part that needs a con-
tinuous flow of love, helps us see the other person with more compassion. We can let go of the pride that sabotages reconciliation.

The exercises that follow are intended to help you get in touch with
how it feels to turn off the flow of love, to give you an opportunity to
practice staying in unconditional mode, and to help you see how the
processes can be used in your relationship to love unconditionally
even in upsetting situations. Without doing the exercises below in

a heartfelt manner (and ultimately applying them), no amount of wisdom or stimulating information will affect your ability to love unconditionally. You need practice in order to model it and inspire those around you to unconditionally love themselves. The examples will demonstrate the typical ways partners go into conditional mode with each other. These must be unlearned. What is in the way for most people is pride, fear, or both. Pride screams, *I am right!* Fear begs not to be rejected. Instead, there has to be a desire to stay connected and in unconditional mode.

There are two effective scenarios you can learn for handling every upsetting situation. Process A is for when you're the one who's upset or angry. Process B is for when your partner is upset or angry. These two processes can be applied to a myriad of situations and relationships. You have a chance to practice and learn them by applying them in Scenarios 1 through 4. (Remember, reestablishing harmony—not being proven right—is your primary aim. The issues will resolve themselves once harmony is reestablished.)

Process A: You Are the One Who's Upset

1. Keep from walking away or shutting down.
2. Take your partner's hand.
3. Look into your partner's eyes.
4. Acknowledge that you love your partner and that there is a problem.
5. Ask if your partner knows why you are upset, then listen and mirror your partner's point of view.
6. Communicate your issue and point of view patiently and lovingly.

Process B: Your Partner Is the One Who's Upset

1. Ask your partner to stay if he or she starts to leave.
2. Ask to take your partner's hand.
3. Look into your partner's eyes.
4. Say, "I know you're upset and I want to talk about it. I love you. I am sorry I upset you."
5. Listen and acknowledge your partner's point of view.
6. Communicate your point of view compassionately.

Practice applying Processes A and B to everyday situations and disagreements by taking yourself through the following examples:

Scenario 1

You upset your partner, and instead of talking it out, your partner walks away from you. Close your eyes and think about how you feel. (I'm guessing it's not a good feeling.) Think about and become aware of what your past automatic reaction has been, then start to go through Process B. Ask your partner not to walk away, take your partner's hands, look into each other's eyes, and without pride say, "I know you're upset and I want to talk about it. I love you. I'm sorry I made you upset and I know we can work this out. I would like to know how you feel about what just happened and then I will tell you how I feel. I would like to know what you would have done differently and I will tell you what I would have done. We can discuss this, both giving our opinions, until we come to an agreement. How do you feel about what just happened?" Remember to use mirroring!

Now, imagine how your partner feels when you get upset and walk away. Your partner is hurt, just as you would be. Remember that you're hurting your partner when you walk away from a conflict. Use Process A when you are upset to stay connected and unconditional.

How did you feel imagining Scenario 1? Did you get a sense that resolution was possible using Processes A and B? Did it bring up more questions? Practicing with Scenarios 2, 3, and 4 will help you find the answers.

Let's move on.

Scenario 2

You upset your partner and you want to establish physical contact by holding hands, but your partner moves away. How do you feel? How can you encourage an emotional environment in which your partner welcomes your touch? Apply Process B and say without pride, "I know you're upset and don't want me to touch you. I love you. I am sorry I made you upset." Then say, "Please take my hand. I know we can work this out together." Continue with the rest of Process B.

Now, imagine how your partner feels when you don't allow yourself to be touched. You partner feels hurt, too.

From here, apply Process A: when you find yourself recoiling from your partner's touch during conflict, stop and try to become aware of what is generating that reaction. Remind yourself of the love you share and reciprocate by taking your partner's hand. Then, continue to follow Process A.

How did it feel to work through the issue in a loving, connected environment?

Scenario 3

You just upset your partner, and instead of talking it out your partner starts yelling at you. You can't even get a word in. What do you feel? Instead of yelling back or shutting down and accepting this distancing behavior, how can you engage your partner in productive communication? Turn to your partner and say without pride, "I know when you get upset that you raise your voice. You're probably not even aware that you do it or how uncomfortable it makes me feel. I am sorry I upset you. Please lower your voice or take a few minutes to cool off so we can discuss it." Continue with the second step and say, "Please take my hand," and then proceed with the rest of Process B.

Put the shoe on the other foot and imagine how your partner feels when you yell. Apply Process A so that when you find yourself yelling, stop and become aware of the automatic behaviors you fall back on. Say to your partner, "I am sorry for raising my voice," or, "I don't want to yell, so I need a few minutes to cool off." Continue to follow Process A.

You may be wondering how you can stop yourself or your partner from yelling in the first place. The answer is that, initially, you can't do either. People who are used to raising their voices will do it automatically and you can't respond until it happens. So, in these scenarios, it is your response to yelling (either yours or your partner's) and your own awareness of what triggers that response that will eventually create change and break the distancing pattern. It may be difficult to realize that the only thing you can really control is your own behavior, but remember that controlling your reactions and responding with love will help your partner to modify his or her behavior, grow awareness, and cultivate an unconditionally loving environment.

Scenario 4

You just upset your partner, and instead of talking and listening to your point, your partner is constantly interrupting you. How does this make you feel? How can you encourage your partner to want to listen to your point of view rather than interrupt you? Again, apply Process B. The first step is to say without pride, "I know you're upset and don't want to hear what I have to say. I love you. I am sorry I made you upset." Continue through the rest of Process B.

Remember a time that you interrupted your partner. Imagine how your partner must have felt. Apply Process A and when you find yourself interrupting, become aware of that tendency, its triggers, and make a conscious decision to stop. Say, "I am sorry for interrupting you." Continue to follow through the rest of Process A.

How did it feel to choose to stay disconnected at the beginning of each exercise? Did you feel hurt, frustrated, confused, angry, or lonely? Were these feelings added to whatever the original problem was? By going into conditional mode, as you can now see, the climate for resolving a problem can quickly deteriorate. In each example there was a problem, negative feelings were exacerbated by conditional behavior, and the conflict quickly escalated. But by using Processes A and B, you can stay in unconditional mode, allowing the positive feelings to dissipate the negative. Did you see and feel how the environment changed? The changed environment is what encourages solutions.

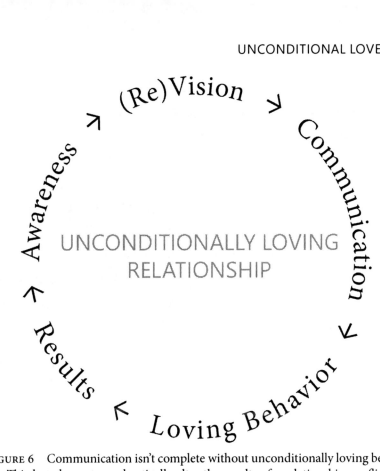

FIGURE 6   Communication isn't complete without unconditionally loving behavior. This last element can drastically alter the results of a relationship conflict for the better.

The examples I've presented for staying in unconditional mode are aimed at overcoming the established patterns of distancing. Its effects may have already taken root and grown into a fixture in your relationship. Fortunately, neurobiological brain research has discovered that the patterns can be reversed. The neuropathways that guide our automatic behaviors can be rewired with practice.[1] We *can* drop habits that have served their purposes and make new ones that suit our visions. Finding solutions requires your continued awareness

---

1. Doidge, Norman, *The Brain That Changes Itself: Stories of Personal Triumph from the Frontiers of Brain Science* (New York: Viking, 2007).

and desire to stay in unconditional mode, so practice Processes A and B until those behaviors take root, grow, and become your normal, everyday behavior.

Becoming unconditionally loving can be a long and difficult process—and the truth is that it never ends because we must always practice it. Painful feelings can discourage us from addressing problems, but it's important to remember that time can't heal all wounds. The hurtful feelings only accumulate and the eggshells we walk on pile up. Going into conditional mode never solves the problem, but loving unconditionally by applying Processes A and B can prevent a problem from building up in the first place.

PART III

01101100 01101111 01110110 0110

00101 01101100 01101111 0111011

Marriage is a commitment—a decision to do, all through life, that which will express your love for your spouse.

– HERMAN KIEVAL

0 01100101 01101100 01101111 01110110 01100101 01101100 01101111 01110110 01100101 011011

IN REAL LIFE: MAKING LOVE WORK

In this chapter, I will describe real-life situations that some of my clients faced, and I will challenge you to consider how you would have responded in their place. Go through the whole process using the tools we've discussed: awareness, vision, and communication. I'll explain how the conflict was resolved at the end of each story, but going through it on your own first gives you a chance to put what you've been reading into practice. When you are prompted, I encourage you to pause, consider what your approach would be, and write down some of your thoughts before continuing.

Betty and Jim

Let's look at an example of a relationship that's missing the tools it needs to succeed. Betty was looking for love in her thirties and met Jim, a sweet, free-spirited man. Jim swept Betty off her feet and they married.

Jim was moving from one job to another, not quite finding himself. Betty, on the other hand, was making a name for herself in her field, achieving the commensurate titles and raises. Soon, it was decided that Jim would stay home and take care of their young children. It wasn't long before conflicts arose.

Betty had become used to being an aggressive go-getter at work because, as a woman, she had to be more assertive and persistent in sharing her ideas compared to the men around her. Once she got home, that habit was difficult to switch off and she found herself acting like the boss to her husband. She was unable to compromise, listen compassionately, or show appreciation to the extent that Jim needed.

Jim began to feel taken for granted, belittled, and neglected. In addition, he grew jealous of his wife's career success, her camaraderie with her co-workers, and the appreciation she received from her superiors for her innovative ideas. He began wanting to go back to work and achieve those things himself. They fought about who was head of the household and who made the financial decisions. Friction arose in the marriage, and they found themselves unequipped with the tools to understand each other's point of view and work through their problems.

Pause for a few moments and imagine yourself as either Jim or Betty. How would you address this conflict? This is a good opportunity for you to put what you've learned about awareness, vision, and communication into practice before applying it to your own relationship. After you've taken a little while to go through the process yourself, I'll walk you through how I helped Jim and Betty repair their relationship and strengthen their bond.

How you would approach this problem using the tools and ideas that you've learned?

I spent a few sessions with Jim and Betty developing their awareness so they could clarify the core issues at work and recognize their needs and desires for their relationship. Once their eyes were open, the cure was to develop a new, thoughtful vision for the relationship. Although they were both skeptical about the value of a vision, they complied.

They wrote their own visions and then compared notes. To their surprise, they discovered they were in agreement in many respects. They both wanted a nurturing, loving, supportive, and affectionate relationship. Discussing it made them realize they'd actually had that type of relationship in the past and there was no reason that, with a little creative, out-of-the-box thinking and hard work, they couldn't have it again.

Next, they created a shared vision for their relationship, one they could own and work toward together. They discussed and agreed on parenting approaches, finances, and spending quality time with each other. These areas had caused most of their past conflicts and had never been satisfactorily resolved. After they wrote their visions for each area and realized with a bit of coaching that compromise was essential for progress, they arrived at a mutual vision they could be happy with. (It's important to note that a strong, functional vision is generally one where both partners feel they have to give in or compromise more than they'd like.)

Jim and Betty came to understand that communication and compromise were essential to realizing their vision, and that they wanted to make loving conversation a top priority in their relationship. They agreed to disconnect the TV, laptops, and smartphones after the kids went to bed so they could reconnect with each other. They asked each other about their day and then helped each other unwind. They both listened with interest and appreciation. Awareness, vision, and communication, as well as their inherent ability and desire to love each other unconditionally, won the day.

John and Marlene

Let's examine the struggles and recovery of another couple. John is a hardworking craftsman who married Marlene and fathered three beautiful children. His job in the city didn't pay well enough for his wife Marlene to stay home to take care of their children, so he worked evenings and weekends at his second job in the suburbs. The second job paid much better than the first, and after a while John saved enough money to buy a family home. It wasn't in great condition, so little by little, with whatever money and time was available, John started to fix the house.

As the years passed, it looked like all his hard work was paying off. His family had a beautiful home. The kids were doing well in school and planning to go to college. John was proud of the fruits of his labor. But throughout all this, Marlene felt increasingly restless and unsatisfied with how much time John spent away from home working. She asked him to cut back to reasonable hours, but her approach was impatient and angry, and she didn't understand what John was trying to accomplish. John, instead of feeling appreciated for being a great provider, only heard accusations that he was an inattentive husband and father. John tried to explain to Marlene that since she didn't work, he would only be able to cut back on his hours once their girls were out of college. He said this with anger, though, so Marlene was hurt and she understood John to mean that her request was unreasonable and not an option.

As John and Marlene got increasingly defensive, misunderstandings arose, communication stopped, and the conflict spiraled until love was cut off from both sides. The situation festered and John and Marlene started to doubt each other's love. Encouraged by her friends, Marlene filed for divorce.

How you would approach this problem using the tools and ideas that you've learned?

John and Marlene started to address their communication issues by practicing the mirroring technique. It's very important to note that they started by discussing topics that were not very contentious—whose turn it was to do the dishes or who got to choose the movie that night—rather than the issue of John's work schedule. By practicing with smaller, less emotionally charged topics, they could focus on the technique without communication spiraling into an argument. Resolving smaller issues also dissolved much resentment, which was a sore spot in the relationship and fed their larger issues.

Soon, they were ready to discuss the core problem of John's work-life balance and Marlene's desire to have him home more often. Mirroring helped both of them to really listen to what the other partner was saying. Each partner realized that the other often made sense and that there was no need to get defensive. As they practiced mirroring and took turns as the sender, they realized that truly feeling heard made them feel loved and brought them closer together.

Marlene realized that John needed to hear appreciation for his hard work, and John realized that Marlene simply missed him and wanted more time together. They recognized that the issues came from very loving intentions on both sides. This revelation allowed them to work together as a team to create a plan based on one question: what would have to happen in order for John to be able to cut back his work hours? They created a tighter budget to eliminate needless spending on non-essentials, and they decided that Marlene could provide another source of income by getting a part-time job. Marlene had always liked retail and interacting with customers. She found a position after only a few weeks.

John and Marlene learned that trying to speak over each other without listening caused needless strife. Once they were willing to work together for the benefit of the relationship, they were able to create solutions that made them happy. It took hard work but they got better at it, and the result was that Marlene and John felt like they were a team, each contributing financially and creating a future together as a couple.

Mastering Life

What's at stake here is the mastery of life. No matter what we embark on, we want to become as good at it as possible. It gives us great satisfaction to excel at something, whether it is having a great sense of humor cultivated by watching comedies and trying out quips to amuse others or being a good cook by attempting many recipes. It also feels good to have people respond to that mastery. Mastery requires time and practice but produces real rewards, and this is especially true when mastering the way we conduct ourselves and interact with others, like John and Marlene did. Mastery means bringing the best out of yourself and others. It means feeling consistently good about yourself and helping others feel that way, too. Loving yourself, being an effective listener and communicator, thinking before acting (particularly in relationships), and being aware of feelings (yours and others') so as to respond appropriately is, without question, the ultimate gift you can give yourself.

The good news is that the ideas presented in this book have consistently worked. That means that you now have tools and concepts to love unconditionally, and the only missing ingredients are totally in your control—time and effort to practice what you have learned.

My organization, The Human Development Company, is here to help you on this magnificent journey. Go to our website (www.thdc. org) and join a growing community of couples and families learning and sharing new ideas about what makes love eternal.

IN REAL LIFE:
YOUR MOVIE LIBRARY

I want to leave you with an additional exercise you and your partner can do together to further develop your toolkit in a fun and productive way. A three-year study recently concluded that the divorce rate was cut in half for newlyweds who watched and discussed movies featuring couples dealing with common relationship issues.[1] The couples chose movies from a provided list and then answered a set of questions. I'd like to provide you with a similar exercise with the questions tailored to reflect the theory and tools I've developed over the last thirty years.

Here's how it works. Pick a movie from the following pages (or choose your own), pop some popcorn, and snuggle up for a cozy night in. When the movie's over, discuss the corresponding questions. Although I've focused on romantic relationships so far in this book, partners and relationships can take many forms, like siblings, parents and children, co-workers, in-laws, and friends. For example, the film *Warrior* credits the actors of the two brothers first, but their

---

1. Ronald D. Rogge, Rebecca J. Cobb, Erika Lawrence, Matthew D. Johnson, Thomas N. Bradbury, "Is Skills Training Necessary for the Primary Prevention of Marital Distress and Dissolution? A 3-Year Experimental Study of Three Interventions," *Journal of Consulting and Clinical Psychology* 81, no. 6 (Dec 2013): 949–961, doi: 10.1037/a0034209.

relationships with their father is worth studying, as is the relationship between Joel Edgerton's character and his wife. Keep an eye out in each of these movies for relationships that resemble those in your life, and then journal your observations using the corresponding questions in this book.

So, dim the lights and let's get started!

Before Sunset (2004)
Julie Delpy and Ethan Hawke

The Five-Year Engagement (2012)
Emily Blunt and Jason Segel

Pariah (2011)
Adepero Oduye and Kim Wayans

The Money Pit (1986)
Tom Hanks and Shelley Long

The Kids Are All Right (2010)
Annette Bening and Julianne Moore

What's Eating Gilbert Grape (1993)
Johnny Depp and Leonardo DiCaprio

Saving Face (2004)
Joan Chen and Michelle Krusiec

The Best Man Holiday (2013)
Morris Chestnut and Taye Diggs

This Is 40 (2012)
Leslie Mann and Paul Rudd

Adrift (2009)
Vincent Cassel and Laura Neiva

Like Water for Chocolate (1992)
Lumi Cavazos and Marco Leonardi

Date Night (2010)
Steve Carell and Tina Fey

The Vicious Kind (2009)
Adam Scott and Brittany Snow

Departures (2008)
Ryoko Hirosue and Masahiro Motoki

Friends with Kids (2011)
Adam Scott and Jennifer Westfeldt

Gun Hill Road (2011)
Esai Morales and Harmony Santana

Whale Rider (2002)
Keisha Castle-Hughes and Rawiri Paratene

Warrior (2011)
Joel Edgerton and Tom Hardy

Silver Linings Playbook (2012)
Bradley Cooper and Jennifer Lawrence

Love and Basketball (2000)
Omar Epps and Sanaa Lathan

Hook (1991)
Dustin Hoffman and Robin Williams

Frozen (2013)
Kristen Bell and Idina Menzel

Questions for Thought and Discussion

1. What were the characters aware of in themselves and in their partners? What were they unaware of?
2. How did characters' visions (conscious or subconscious) affect their relationships with their partners? What vision would you create instead?
3. Are the characters ever unloving or conditional with each other? How could they be more loving and unconditional?
4. How do the characters handle conflict? Does communication break down? Do they stay loving? How does this compare to your relationships?
5. How do the characters communicate with each other? Do they ever blame each other or jump to conclusions? How does this compare to your relationship? How would you improve their communication?
6. Did the characters love themselves unconditionally? How did the characters struggle to balance loving themselves and

loving their partners? How does this compare to your experience?

7. Did the partners in each relationship seem to have similar expectations for the relationship? Were they open about their expectations with each other? How does their experience compare to yours?

THE HUMAN DEVELOPMENT COMPANY

0 01100101 01101100 01101111 01110110 01100101 01101100 01101111 01110110 01100101 011011

The Human Development Company is an educational research organization built on the Continuum Theory of Human Development, a superordinate theory that gives a clear road map to developing the full potential of every human being. THDC staff consists of highly educated professionals working on several applications of Stefan Deutsch's theory of love and human development:

1. *Saving A Marriage—Saves A Family* is a national campaign to reduce divorce in America by twenty percent by the year 2020. Divorce rips families apart, generates emotional hardships for children from which many never recover, creates financial hardships, and disrupts a child's ability to thrive in school. Couples in committed relationships attend webinars and live events to learn how to safeguard their relationships.

2. SELFS is a K–12 school curriculum based on a new model of human development that teaches students, parents, and teachers the tools espoused in this book: awareness, vision, communication, and unconditionally loving behavior.

3. REAL is a student-led university and college resident life program that promotes self-esteem, interpersonal relationships, and unconditionally loving behavior towards self and others.

4. THDC Training Institute trains psychotherapists and other counseling professionals in Deutsch's unique and highly successful approach to helping patients heal themselves and their significant relationships. As of September 2015, the couple's therapy program has entered the beta-testing phase. If interested, please e-mail president@thdc.org.

5. Love2Care is a wellness program for healthcare professionals and company staff that integrates the latest medical science of stress management and wellness with Deutsch's latest science of self-care and self-love. It was developed by Deutsch and a team of medical doctors. If interested in bringing this program to your hospital, company, or organization, contact president@thdc.org.

6. Parenting a Victor teaches parents to do the one thing they are sure they do but unintentionally do not: be unconditionally loving, even when the young child, teenager, or adult child disappoints, hurts, or angers them—something more important to a child's health, happiness, and success in life than any Harvard education or sports scholarship. Look for Deutsch's forthcoming book on parenting.

7. LifePro™ is an educational initiative to help the baby boomer generation perceive the aging process as one of power and promise rather than decline. Deutsch coined the phrase Life-Pros© to describe such aging individuals who have continued their journeys of growth and who realize that this stage of life was always intended to be the most productive, powerful, and loving. Look for Deutsch's forthcoming book on aging.

8. www.JustSayYesToLove.com is a website that is near completion. Originally intended for singles searching for people

on the path to loving themselves and others uncondtionally (with the awareness, vision, and communication skills required to maintain great relationships), the site is expanding to include couples and people looking for friendships. As of September 2015, access is free and people can use the questionnaires to enrich their understanding of themselves and what constitutes a potentially good fit.

Prior to founding The Human Development Company, Stefan Deutsch co-founded Impact on Hunger, Inc., which became the educational umbrella arm of the entire US hunger community, including UNICEF. Impact on Hunger produced the first hunger education curriculum for grades K–12, funded by AID. Its projects included Patrick's Walk (an endeavor blessed by the pope), a two-year partnership campaign with Muhammad Ali, and the US's first food collection, Hunger Awareness Day, at the NY Mets Shea Stadium.

In time, Deutsch came to understand that the hunger Impact was addressing was merely a symptom of something else. Determined to address the root cause of hunger and unhappiness, he followed his theoretical search to conclude it was our fear-based inability to unconditionally love ourselves and others preventing human beings from reaching our full potential. With unconditional love, it is impossible to be knowingly complicit in others' exploitation, disenfranchisement, and disempowerment.

Over the past twenty years, Deutsch has given talks and workshops for singles, couples, parents, seniors, and therapists, and has taught at major national and international psychotherapy conferences. Now, THDC teaches human beings how to become self-sufficient when it comes to loving themselves, and empowering them to love others unconditionally.

The Human Development Company is always looking to connect with those who are interested in its theories and approaches. If you are interested in learning more about THDC or becoming involved with one of its programs, visit www.thdc.org for more information or email president@thdc.org to connect with a program director.

If you enjoyed
LOVE DECODED
read the theory it is based on

THE
CONTINUUM
THEORY

OF HUMAN DEVELOPMENT

by Stefan Deutsch

INTRODUCTION

The task is . . . not so much to see what no one has seen; but to think what nobody has yet thought, about that which everybody sees.

– ERWIN SCHRÖDINGER

s Dr. Richard Lerner explains in *Concepts and Theories of Human Development*, "Alternative world views lead us to ask different questions about development. Not better, just different. The real value of a new worldview and the theories it may bring forth is in its usefulness for descriptions, how well it explains development, and its use in devising new ways to optimize human behavior."[1]

The Continuum Theory™ provides just such a worldview, a new definition of life span and human development, which more fully explains human development and opens up new worlds of possibility for reaching the optimum potential of each and every individual.

The concepts for the Continuum Theory were developed away from mainstream academia. After I obtained my bachelor's degree in physics and philosophy, I had a hard time with the philosophy of psychology, so I left NYU's Graduate School where I was studying movement therapy. Although Freud's concepts were intuitive and well ahead of his time, I felt uncomfortable with the idea of building a science on them. It felt like a lot of the terminology was without strict, functional definitions, and I took issue with the convoluted imagery of the struggle between the ego, id, and superego, and the Oedipal Complex into which all problems had to fit. Jung, with his concepts of the twelve archetypes and the universal unconscious, was not a better fit for me. The developmental theories which focused primarily on the first ten years of life—the theories of Piaget, Erikson, Vygotsky, Bronfenbrenner, Ainsworth, Watson—all used observation and then developed a statement about that observation. Kant said, "Observation without theory is blind, theory without observation is empty," clearly intimating which has to come first.[2] A theory is an intuitive insight into the nature of reality which needs to precede observation, not the other way around (like Schrödinger said, about something everybody sees but nobody has yet thought). Otherwise it is only a statement about an observation and not a theory, in my opinion.

And finally, the main reason I left mainstream academia was because, again in my opinion, if a theory of human development is truly a theory and not just a truism about a set of observable data, we should be able to apply it and get answers to all the issues and problems surrounding human development, not just for people up to age ten or in mid-life, or for dysfunctions, but rather for each and every phase, stage, and issue of life. A theory of human development needs to be able to give life to answers no matter where we look—which I did not see with the present set of theories and still don't, and it is why I decided to search for answers that satisfied these two criteria for me. I placed myself at the margins—and here is what Joseph Melnick wrote about us working at the margins.

> If we believe that growth occurs at the boundary and that remaining marginal in the sense of living in two worlds is the desired stance . . . it follows that we need to look at the positive values of the "irrelevance definition" of marginality. We need to be cautious about embracing too much of the mainstream judgment that if we are not central to the dominant central perspective then we are of limited professional and theoretical value.
>
> When you are marginal, you have the freedom to be more experimental. You are not tied down by the rules and introjects of the prevailing culture. Nor are you governed by bureaucrats who often stifle creativity, replacing it by rigid standards of conduct and practice.
>
> In sum, when pondering the question, "Are we becoming too marginal?" my response is, "Not marginal enough." I believe that our challenge is to hold onto our marginality in the future.[3]

I believe that we continually have to develop universal new ideas and theories for growth and development to occur in any area. This is also true of our ideas of life span, human development, and the self, which are the areas I have been focusing on.

The Continuum Theory

My vision was to establish *nomothetic* laws about human development: laws that focus on universal sequences and their contexts in human development that could apply to all people all of the time.

In the past, we lived on the earth without knowing what Earth was, having ideas like the earth is flat, it's the center of the universe, the sun revolves around us and if it gets angry it may not rise again. We lived with ignorance and misunderstanding. But once we had the knowledge that the earth was round, it inspired us to travel the globe and meet other civilizations. Once we understood that the sun wasn't an angry god that revolved around us, we could stop being afraid that our actions could cause it to not rise again. We could envision traveling in space. These understandings were vital contributions to humanity's growth.

You may ask me if it is important to have a functional definition of self to advance our knowledge in human development, psychology, and psychotherapy. For me, the answer is, absolutely. Can we do what we do in psychology and psychotherapy without knowing what the self is, or agreeing upon a definition of what the self is? To me the answer is, *we certainly have been trying but have not achieved it well enough.* For the science of psychology and psychotherapy, we need to have a functional definition of the self that everyone can agree on, so the research that is done can be uniformly described and understood by everyone.

I have given this close to thirty years of thought, asking questions that perhaps others haven't and not accepting answers that perhaps others have.

The life span development of a human being is evolutionary in nature. I believe it occurs as an overlapping, three-part developmental process: body, mind (brain), and the self. The self is conceived-birthed along with body and mind, with all three existing initially as potential that is able to develop fully. All three begin this development at conception-birth. The self has the identical potential for development as the body and mind and is fully integrated with body and mind. The self is the seat of conscious awareness. It is the *I* we refer to. The more fully it is developed, the more it is able to use the body and the mind and its own abilities and facilities to navigate effectively through life.

It makes complete sense that the self would identify itself with what it becomes aware of first, i.e., with its own body. It is the first thing its awareness becomes familiar with, the first thing it experiences, the first thing it can begin to log into its memory bank (the mind), the first thing it can begin to comprehend, and the first thing its parents continually attend to. So, since the self's first conscious experience is of and with its body, it stands to reason it will identify with and believe that it is a body.

As the mind develops, the self begins to notice that those in charge of its development are trying to reach another part of it other than its body. The repetitious nature of much of this early communication is intended for the self to remember certain things like the naming of objects. It begins to realize that it can bring forth, recall this repetitious information, that it is using something else other than its body. It begins to use this other part and finds that it is rewarded with appreciation from those in charge. It begins to enjoy using it. The self may not know yet what this other part is or what it is called, or where the seat of this apparatus, its mind, is. Those attending to it are beginning to teach it language, counting, and the recognition of objects; later, they ask it to memorize facts; and later, they ask it to think about problems of mathematics, reasoning, and consequential thinking. It is natural for the self to start to think of itself as a body and a mind.

Since the concept that we are self (the self being the conscious force that is aware of and makes decisions with relation to its body and mind) is missing from our developmental philosophy, the self's developmental needs are never addressed. Nor does it become fully aware and conscious of its own abilities or facilities. Therefore, the self's needs and developmental potential are left latent or, worse, are damaged and continue to wait to be healed and fully developed.

From conception, each human being has a life force, an energy to potentialize its body, mind, and self. The reality of this life force is obvious when we consider how a zygote potentializes in the womb into a full-blown human being which is birthed. This life force continues throughout life. From conception and on into late teens, each human being's life force, the energy to potentialize, is focused primarily on the full development of the body. Once that is completed, this developmental energy, the life force moving us to develop fully, shifts its energy to the full development of the mind's potential. From late teens to around forty years of age, each human being's life force is focused primarily on the full development of the mind. That is why the questions a human being asks at around age thirteen—What's for dinner? Can I get the latest sneakers?—shift around the age of twenty-plus to more conceptual questions about politics, religion, gender, race, the future, and relationships that requires one to use the mind.

The third stage, which starts around forty years of age, is when nature again shifts its energy from the development of the mind's potential to the full development of the self's potential. This explains not only mid-life crises but also why so many individuals begin to turn from materialism (which is simply the self using the memory bank and calculator that is the brain, quantifying what one has, thinking that more is better, and that more equals happiness) to an awareness, a realization that more is not making oneself, or anyone for that matter, happy. The shift occurs when the questions that are being asked regarding how to achieve happiness change from the quantity of stuff and money to the quality of one's life. One begins to question one's own motives, attitudes, relationships, and career path, thus becoming what we might call a more aware person, and perhaps one who yearns for a more meaningful lifestyle.

Of course, even though going through each stage is part of nature's plan, all but the body stage must be consciously fostered by other human beings. This development of the body stage can be seen when a child will naturally try to stand up, then try to walk, engage in play, and generally try to imitate other bodily movements and actions of adults around him or her. All of this helps growth and development of the body's potential. The same is only true to a limited degree with the mind. A child might acquire language by imitation, but reading and writing must be taught, and problem solving and consequential and creative thinking must be explained at a time the mind is most capable of acquiring these abilities—from twenty years of age onward. The final stage, that of developing and potentializing the self, takes the greatest amount of teaching and conscious attention. We initially teach self-control and certain moral issues to a child and young adult in order to have them be ready to potentialize their self's full development in the third stage, around forty.

Historically, two factors prevented people from potentializing both their minds and their selves. The first was that all their time was consumed by simply trying to find food and protect themselves from dangers.[4] The second was that the average life span was so short, it prevented most people from reaching the chronological age where their life force could shift into either the full development of mind (twenty-plus) or later to the full development of the self (forty-plus). Both of these developmental stages need conscious attention and teaching by those who have developed their own minds and selves. Very few people ever developed their minds beyond learning language, customs, and traditions. There were even fewer people whose selves were developed, who could then help to develop and potentialize others' selves.

When philosophers and psychologists debate about the self, it is always whether there exists some type of solid, full-blown, finished entity like the body or the brain that can be examined and studied. In trying to get a handle on the self, it seems we harken back to ideas we generally think of as spiritual: an immortal soul that persists after the body dies, a being, a spirit (as in guardian spirit), an invisible entity inside of us that usually is ascribed consciousness, and often is synonymous with goodness. We relate to self as a spirit in a similar way that we see a god as a spirit, something that perhaps directs or should direct us.

What seems to be missing from this debate is the possibility that the self is very much like the body and mind, birthed at the same time and totally integrated with body and mind. It is not a separate entity but has different facilities, as do body and mind. I believe all three are vibrating, energetic entities. All three come into existence at birth. All three need nourishment and nurturing. All three have their own developmental potential. For simplicity's sake, I call the various abilities that can be potentialized in the body *muscles*, in the mind *capacities*, and in the self *facilities*.

All three need specific exercises for their specific abilities to fully develop. If you tie up the feet, like some people used to do, you can damage the body's potential for mobility and balance. If you do not talk to a child or engage the mind of a child in reasoning, you will damage the mind's potential to communicate and reason. The self has its own facilities with potential to develop. But since we cannot see self, and since from science's perspective it does not exist, we do not worry about what developmental damage we may be causing by, as it were, tying it up, not nourishing it properly, not exercising it suitably, and not developing it correctly. I believe the facilities of the self are actually diminished and damaged over time instead of being fully developed, which I believe is the primary reason why many people experience emotional problems and feel unsatisfied and unfulfilled with their lives.

Both Eastern philosophers and Western philosophers and psychologists deny the existence of the self as a real entity. Eastern philosophers like Confucius and Lao Tzu were hoping to end humanity's suffering caused by what they saw as attachment to self (ego) and its struggle with accepting the way things were (which is not that different from teachings about being rewarded in the afterlife if you accept the way things are here on Earth). Western philosophers and psychologists denied the existence of the self because they couldn't observe or study the self. I believe that the denial of self as a real entity is a mistake of major proportions.

Since our origin, humans have looked up and have seen light coming from the sky. One was a very bright, warm light, and one was a smaller, cooler light, and there were lots of tiny glimmering lights. We didn't know where any of these lights were coming from; all we knew was that we could observe the light. The observing of the light was real, even though the source was obscure. Later, much later, we were able to establish the source and the composition of the sun, moon, and stars, and explain why they emanated or reflected light. Knowing the composition of the source of the observable light isn't necessary for us to say that the light we observe is real and therefore its source is real. I believe it is same with self.

We have for thousands of years observed behavior, which we have attributed to a part of a human being that isn't the body or mind. We have called it *spirit*, *soul*, and *being*. It has been clear to us that a person who goes around slums, gathering up and caring for the dead and dying, is not behaving based on a well-developed body or super-intelligent mind. We understand this behavior is being activated by another part of the person. We have observed this type of *selfless* behavior in many individuals historically and close to home. We have created words in our languages to describe it. But because we can't observe the source of this selfless behavior, like we couldn't observe the source of the lights in the sky, and because we don't know the source's origin and composition, we are trying to dismiss the reality of the source, while accepting the reality of the behavior.

The concept of atoms, which was put forth by Democritus in the third millennium BCE as "tiny, invisible, indivisible particles that in different combinations formed all material reality," was similarly ignored and discredited by our much more famous philosophers like Aristotle, Plato, Socrates, Kant, Newton, and Galileo, who all believed matter was made up the four elements: air, fire, earth, and water. Why? It was taught by wise, educated men in power who had control over what people believed and, no matter how logical and intuitively correct the theory was, at that time they could not see atoms.

We can't see the self. So, what? Now, I don't think that it is all bad to not believe in things we can't see, like the Loch Ness Monster, Leprechauns, and Superman, but when our *experience* continually confirms a concept, we owe it to ourselves to investigate it more fully.

There is actual harm done to a person because we insist on denying the existence of a developmental self. This harm relates directly to all the issues that have the prefix *self*: low self-esteem, no self-support, no self-confidence, no self-love, low self-worth, no self-respect, no self-awareness, no self-care, not self-motivated. They translate into terms such as self-destructive, unconscious, unaware, self-conscious, self-doubt, self-sabotage, procrastination.

Many of the issues of psychology, parenting, education, and medicine (such as stress, anxiety, depression, personal failure, and rebellion), can be explained and healed better by viewing the self as an entity that can make good decisions once it is fully developed. This development is based on 1) growing its awareness so it can be fully in touch with what feels painful, wrong, or absent; 2) being able to clearly define pain, as well as wants and needs, which we call creating a vision; 3) communicating these newly recognized feelings and needs effectively and without blame; and 4) doing it all with unconditional, loving behavior. Self-love prompts one to obtain what one needs. Self-love is synonymous with self-sufficiency, not with being selfish or self-centered. Since loving energy is nourishment like air, food, and water, it makes logical sense that it needs to be supplied unconditionally. The conditional behavior of most well-meaning parents, friends, and others deprives people of the necessary amount of nourishment they need to thrive. The best solution is what I mentioned before—teaching children to become unconditionally self-sufficient, as they are in acquiring air, food, and water.

The Story of M: Her Father's Condition

The father of one of my associates (we'll call her Mary) had a severe spinal injury when she was just a child. The accident not only paralyzed him from the neck down but also forced him to live in an iron lung, in an institution for the rest of his life. His wife, left with two children, asked if it would be all right to divorce him and remarry. He agreed. Then, a choice had to be made by this unfortunate man: to live a life of purpose, or to feel sorry for himself for what turned out to be another forty years. Forty years of life with a well-educated brain and a body that could not be used to take care of himself.

Tragedy strikes many individuals. Some tragedies—like bank-ruptcies, job loss, divorce, fires that destroy homes, robberies, car accidents, and serious but not deadly illnesses—are not nearly as cat-astrophic as being stuck in an iron lung because, one may argue, they comparatively allow for greater possibility of reclaiming one's life.

Many individuals who experience these tragedies are healthy, well-educated people. The rest of their lives is still in front of them and they have a clear possibility of seizing an opportunity to con-front their tragedy and overcome it. And yet many of them become depressed, non-functioning, bitter, angry, self-pitying, defeated, un-happy individuals.

What is the difference between those who choose the road to overcoming tragedy and those who feel defeated?

Mary's father—who had lost his body, who needed help even for the most personal and potentially embarrassing bodily functions, and who was locked into an iron lung in one room—made a choice. He became one of the most prolific lobbyists for all forms of dis-abilities and inspired legislation and reforms and raised America's consciousness regarding the needs of the disabled.

The stress, the hopelessness that tragedies and disappointments produce affect individuals who are both physically and mentally well-developed, differently. Why should that be if we are only a body and a brain? If we are only a body and a brain, then all the answers and solutions must lie in those two areas, the only areas open for investigation and research.

Focusing on body and mind has led to medical and psychological communities prescribing drugs that numb feelings or induce a sense of euphoria (well-being). Both affect the body's and brain's function-ing. While in some cases they may assist the individual to temporar-ily function better day to day, they in no way assist in dealing with the underlying causes of why the tragedy affected a person in such a debilitating way.

Looking for and trying to deal with underlying causes is the province of some form of psycho-intervention. Psychiatry is depending more and more on drugs. It has no other model for effective intervention. The time taken by psychiatrists for conversation is lessening, according to the *New York Times*.[5] Even when they understand the background of a client, the client doesn't necessarily feel better about themselves or the future. The results of talk are meager.

What part of a human being is preventing this healthy, well-developed body and this healthy, well-developed brain from functioning in the same healthy way it used to before the tragedy occurred? After all, it is the same body and same brain! What part is in control of this body and brain?

My belief is that without having something real to work with, something that we know must be at the root of emotional distress, we cannot approach healing effectively. Including in our scientific model the concept of a real self—a real self that has been damaged in childhood or adulthood and now needs rehabilitation and development—would make diagnosis, prognosis, and treatment more likely to succeed.

We know without needing to do tests that the self's four areas of development (which I will discuss later) have been ignored or damaged and need to be the focus of attention. Developing clients' awareness so they can be aware of their full spectrum of feelings, rather than numbing their awareness of pain with drugs, is the start.

The next step is to teach clients about the need for creating a new vision, a new set of possibilities. Once clients understand that they can affect the future by implementing a new vision, they become more hopeful. Even if they don't believe in it, their focus of attention becomes the future with positive possibilities. In *The Mind and the Brain*, Dr. Jeffrey M. Schwartz and Sharon Begley discuss the brain's plasticity and how vision can require the use one's brain.[6]

Teaching individuals about effective communication helps their vision begin the manifesting process. Once we communicate to the people in our universe, the universe and people begin to respond to our communications. The communication creates something to talk about, a future with possibilities.

Finally, teaching people to love and ask for love, the necessary nourishment of the self, gives them energy to persist. Instead of drugs, what people need is to learn to love (feed) themselves. Exactly the way they learned how to feed their bodies and brains with air-food-water, they will learn to feed themselves with love.

The most hopeful, energizing thing in life is to have a vision that is fed by love. At the time of conceptualizing the Continuum Theory, I hypothesized that what we call love is a form of nourishment that nourishes the self. Since then, the research of Barbara Fredrickson at the University of North Carolina has made significant strides toward proving my thesis that love is exactly like air, food, and water, nourishment vital to the development and thriving of human beings.

At this time, mainstream therapeutic interventions do not address love as a real, tangible energy. Harville Hendrix has written about getting, keeping, and giving love. His program, Imago Relationship Therapy, has been highly successful, although it lacks the theoretical underpinnings of what love is. Its success can be directly related to an approach that emphasizes what my theory calls loving behavior. Empathy, respect, validation, consideration, patience, and conscious communication are all different forms of love, different ways of transmitting loving energy. They all nourish that part of us that is not the body or brain but the self, which controls both body and brain.

My therapeutic training is in Gestalt therapy, which is highly awareness oriented, and the connection between therapist and client often will include the touching of hands, hugs, cradling as an infant, and many other loving behaviors that are not encouraged in most other therapeutic interventions. Yet, Gestalt theory never mentions love and insists that the self is merely a process of ebb and flow—not very useful for either the therapist or the client.

The issue isn't or shouldn't be whether the self is real or not. The issue is or should be what explains human behavior in a way that is consistent with our experience, is more useful in positively altering human behavior and thereby assisting individuals in achieving their life goals and living happy, healthy lives. Ease of access is another issue: which explanation is more easily understood by the layperson and clinician alike, and can more easily be used by all for the betterment of society? Imagine having scientific ideas of human development and the development of the self that inspires laypeople, one they can learn and effectively use themselves, just like they could use the wheel or arithmetic.

My mission was to create a theory of who we are and how we can create better lives, a theory that is easily learned and easily used by everyone. First, I spent over ten years devising a new theory of life span and human development. Then, I spent the next twenty years researching the many applications of the theory, all of which turned out to support its efficacy. So, for me, the debate about whether self is an entity has been over for quite a while.

For you perhaps, the debate is just starting. I am more than happy to take on your skepticism, your questions, and your objections.

Self is an entity, albeit not defined in the way philosophy and psychology often try to define an entity as separate, solid, visible, or taking up space. I believe that the reason we are still embroiled in the debate of whether self is real, besides the fact that I have not yet made my theory or findings fully public, is that we keep starting the debate by going all the way back to the Cartesian theater and before, continually asking the same questions rather than new, practical ones. Actually, the questions and answers haven't changed much—only the vocabulary for expressing them has, much of it now coming from clinical psychology.

New Questions

My experience some thirty years ago with Creative Aging, an organization I co-founded, was that people resisted the idea of aging. They did not have the perspective that each year, each decade brought the possibility of developing a yet undeveloped potential—a potential which, once developed, would assure greater power and satisfaction in life. I researched this by asking hundreds of individuals to chart life on a graph. The result was a bell-shaped curve, peaking at thirty-five years of age, clearly showing that the overwhelming majority of people perceived life span as an inevitably declining process. This perception is quite evident when we see people turning thirty, forty, and fifty, who by and large are upset and anxious rather than enthusiastically looking forward to the next decade of their lives and development.

Why is this? I wondered.

Are they correctly perceiving life? Is their definition of life as an inevitably declining process turning it into one exactly, like a self-fulfilling prophecy? What if it turned out that life span was actually an upward-curving, ever-potentializing process? If that were true, would people forty, fifty, and sixty years of age perceive the next decade of their lives differently? And if that were possible (that life is an upward-curving process of potentializing), what theoretical framework would support it and prove it? My intuition said that, in fact, life is an upward-curving process of potentializing, which we misperceive because the body and, to a lesser degree, the brain do seem to decline with age. If we believe we are only body and brain, then we are right to resist this process and not look forward to the next decade and then the next. After all, who in their right mind (or left brain) wants to watch themselves decline?

I set out to find a theoretical framework that would not only prove that life is an upward-curving process of potentializing, but also in the process, change people's perceptions. I wanted to inspire people across generations to find their true potential, satisfaction, and un-conditional love, and to motivate people to be the most productive in their later years. Retirement, for most, is certainly not the most productive part their lives.

So, with that as background, let's delve into the theory.

The Theory of Self: Research

I believe that psychology need not go, as it does presently, in two different directions: 1) the study of pathology and 2) the study of well-being. I believe that the body and mind, both being machines, can and do break down, can produce variations that are beyond our control and even our imagination, and can lack certain hormones and other chemicals needed for health and well-being. But I believe that these cases are by far in the minority. As far as the causes of de-pression, anxiety, and other mental illnesses medical and psychology communities are attempting to cure, I believe that most of the pa-thologies are the result of the same dynamic that applies to a majori-ty of individuals: a basic ignorance of who they are as human beings, how they function, their lack of awareness of what their needs truly are, their lack of vision and knowledge as to how to ask for what they want, and finally, how to be unconditionally loving toward themselves (self-sufficiency) and others, and how to ask for and receive unconditionally loving behavior.[7]

This can all be taught! It can happen once people understand that they have a self that needs development and rehabilitation.

I believe that both an individual life span and human evolution (at least from the Stone Age through today) have three-part developmental processes: the physical, the mental, and that of the self. The micro-evolutionary process (or human development and life span) mirrors the macro-evolutionary process of human evolution. Both theories are easy for people to follow and for me to provide evidence for. I will start with the theory of human evolution, because the historical documentation makes it relatively simple to prove.

The three stages of human evolution can be seen when we document the evolution of ideas relating to the body/me survival stage, the mind/we survival stage, and the self/us survival stage. It is this theory of human evolution that underscores my theory of life span.

Although I am not an archaeologist or anthropologist, records seem to indicate that the Paleolithic Age, or the Old Stone Age, covered about ninety-nine percent of human history. During this period, stone tools were developed. During the Paleolithic Age, humans grouped together in small scale societies and gathered plants and hunted wild animals. This ninety-nine percent of human history took more than two million years. Human beings lived in isolated bands with the average life expectancy of perhaps twenty years or less. The next stage in human evolution was called the Pleistocene, and it was characterized by the introduction of agriculture around the tenth millennium BCE.

When you consider that, for nearly two million years, human beings existed in a very primitive mode of survival, don't you have to ask yourself the question, *Why?* I did!

We see how rapidly knowledge advances today. Then, why did it take nearly two million years for humanity to move from stone tools to metals, from exclusively hunting and gathering to also developing the knowledge of domesticating plants and animals when their very survival was at stake?

Anthropologists have theories about why this took so long to happen, and so do I. The following table can start to explain my theory.[8]

Humans by Era and Region	Average Lifespan at Birth (years)
Late Pleistocene (Neanderthals)	20
Upper Paleolithic	33
Neolithic	20
Bronze Age	18
Classical Greece	20–30
Classical Rome	20–30
Pre-Columbian North America	25–35
Medieval Britain	20–30
Early Twentieth Century	30–40
Current world average	78

According to the Encyclopedia Britannica

Certainly, humans being in small groups isolated from one another, fearful of and hostile to one another and focusing on daily survival, was a contributing factor to their inability to develop better survival tools and ideas. As for those in warmer parts of the world with an abundance of easily accessible animals and vegetables, perhaps they did not need to develop tools or ideas for survival. But I believe there was an even more important factor. And that was their life span.

I believe that peopl do not develop their brain's potential for problem solving and consequential thinking until after twenty years of age. And for that to even happen after twenty, the groundwork for thinking, as opposed to mimicking and doing, has to be laid. I believe that not only was the training of individual young limited to survival skills, but also that too few lived long enough to use their own brain's development to analyze their experiences, entertain ideas, and perform trial and error, which could have brought about new solutions. As archeologists have shown, critical, evolutionary thinking happened only in the most limited sense for a very long time.

As we can see by analyzing the table, the short, average life expectancy persisted until the early twentieth century. So, how did humanity manage to create advances in knowledge, given my theory? When people began domesticating plants and animals around ten thousand years ago, disease from domesticated animals and closer contact with denser human populations brought down the average life expectancy. But population numbers went way up. Because of better nutrition, the chances of more people surviving longer was statistically ensured. Survival was no longer tied to what the environment had to offer so much as to hard work or the weather. Agricultural communities also developed specialized trades. This set of circumstances allowed more individuals to reach an age where their brains' potential could be developed, along with having more time, in winter and growing seasons, where the potential of their brains could be put to use.

It is not surprising that with the advent of sewage systems, hygiene, antibiotics, anesthetics, and sufficiently available food in the nineteenth and twentieth centuries, record numbers of people started to live into their forties, fifties, and sixties. And it was these individuals who were directly responsible for industrial revolutions and nearly all of the scientific advances that improved the quality of life.

But that is not all that has happened as a result of scientific advancements leading to longer life spans. Another revolution—that of a morality that included strong social responsibility—started to take root.

Again, how would we explain this by looking at life span? Why were there two world wars and countless others, genocides and holocausts, slavery and child labor, together with all of these scientific advances? After all, didn't we have an ever-growing number of these mind-developed, educated human beings? Isn't developing the mind enough to make people more caring about other human beings? History clearly tells us no. And to this day, merely being educated does not equate with being compassionate and caring. It seems that a developed mind is insufficient for the greater causes of humanity: ending hunger and poverty, bringing peace, and ensuring equality and opportunity for self-expression to all.

The second question you may want to ask yourself is, *Why did it take two million plus another ten thousand years for us to start becoming more morally responsible for our fellow human beings?*

If we go back to the table, we see that today, the average life span is seventy-eight years. At the turn of the twentieth century, it was forty-seven years in the US. In most other countries, it was even less.

The answer is relatively simple. With the majority of human beings living only into their twenties and thirties, not only was there insufficient time to develop the self, but not even sufficient time to develop the mind. Moreover, survival, dominance, and the competitive nature of humanity were at the forefront of human interactions.

At the turn of the twentieth century, more food and then penicillin brought the average life expectancy to forty-seven, and the advent of universal education began to provide the foundation for the wholesale development of people's minds. Air travel, television, atomic energy, medical breakthroughs, the Internet, and many more inventions are the clear product of the millions of human beings now afforded the opportunity to develop their minds. But world wars, religious wars, hunger and starvation, abuse, slave trade, servitude, hate, cold wars, nuclear annihilation, financially using people by not paying or underpaying them, still persisted.

It wasn't until the mid-1950s, when the population started to reach their fifties, sixties, and beyond in large numbers to today's average life expectancy of seventy-eight, that millions of people with developed minds began to reach an age where the full development of their selves was possible. So, it is no coincidence that there has been a greater response to global strife, hunger, and illness that is much more humane and caring than ever before.

1. Love Proves the Self Is Real

I became conscious of the word *love* at about the age of thirteen. It was, of course, in the romantic sense of the word. Since then, I've met thousands of people and have come across very few who have not experienced the pain of love lost, of being rejected by one whom we love.

It is common knowledge that love is wanted and needed by human beings. It is also common knowledge that love can be given and received just like a gift—a little, a lot, or not at all. Just read the books—from romance to self-help, from psychology to spirituali-ty—as they incessantly talk about love. So, is the love that everyone talks about and writes about and believes in fact or fiction?

The sciences, including psychology, have given little attention to the fact that love 1) is wanted and needed and 2) can be given and received by all. Combining logic and experiential observation, I have discovered that what our experience indicates to be true is absolutely correct. These two facts are the foundation for a dramatic shift in our knowledge about human development, the self, and love. These new ideas have a profound impact on psychology, psychotherapy, parent-ing, education, relationships, and especially our views about the self and human development.

Not long ago, it was common knowledge that Earth was the center of the universe. That was fiction. When Galileo proved Copernican heliocentrism (the fact that Earth revolved around the sun), he was denounced and accused of heresy. Why such anger at a new idea? Only a hundred and fifty years ago, the greatest universities on Earth were teaching that air, fire, water, and earth made up everything ma-terial in the universe. Why were they still teaching this, you may ask yourself, when the concept of the atom was put forward over two millennia ago by the philosopher Democritus? The idea of at-oms was considered foolishness. Invisible particles—please! Just like the king's new clothes, fairy tales are for children, not serious adults, certainly not scientists! As we mull over the two examples above, consider what Thomas Kuhn, the father of the modern philosophy of science, had to say about progress in scientific ideas: "normal sci-ence" has a built-in resistance to revolutionary new ideas.[9] As we saw, Democritus and Galileo were, unfortunately, ahead of their time.

The ideas I formulated over thirty years ago about the nature of love were similarly ahead of their time. I believe these ideas will have a dramatic impact on people's quality of life. I believe science today is ready and willing to hear new ideas about love, especially an idea that will change the way the sciences approach human development, which impacts human relationships and, therefore, happiness. At the core of the new approach lies a new theory of the existence of the self. As we have discovered in the past, just because science says something exists or doesn't, doesn't make it so. I do not mean to imply that science hasn't made or won't continue to make a tremendous contribution to the advancement of knowledge and the quality of life. But often, our obsession with the observable, our comfort with what we think we know, and our fear of being wrong, makes us persist and insist on old, ineffective ideas and hinders us from seeing what may be right in front of us.

As far as we know, love is (like *atomos* used to be) not observable—not by x-rays, cathode chambers, certainly not by the human eye. Therefore, to science, it doesn't exist and isn't worthy of study. Yet, it seems to me that the effects of love are very observable and easily replicable in scientific studies. Although there is talk of love everywhere, no scientific theory has ever been put forth regarding the nature of love. This has kept in place the universal confusion about what love is and how to love effectively.

It is not surprising that one of the most commonly used sayings about love is "we hurt the ones we love the most." Look at the high divorce rate between people who pledged eternal love, and consider the lack of closeness in many parent–child relationships. It seems we do hurt the ones we love the most. If this is true, it is obvious that human beings don't know, and aren't being taught, how to love and be loved. I know my theories of the self and the nature of love, which are parts of my Continuum Theory of Human Development, will change that.

After I theorized that life span is a three-stage developmental process—body, mind, and finally self—I wondered: If the self were a real entity, just like the body and brain, what questions would that generate? Since we can't see it, where does it reside? What would nourish it? It must need nourishment exactly like the body and brain do. How would we develop it? It must need a developmental protocol, like the body and brain have. How would it interact with the body and brain? We discovered how the body and brain interact with each other. What would its role be in daily life and in a person's decision-making process?

It was questions like these that took me on a twenty-year quest that ended when the Continuum Theory of Human Development finally had all the pieces of the puzzle in place.

Out of asking some simple questions, which I don't believe I'd ever heard asked before, came more questions, then the answers, one by one. One of the hardest answers to come up with, one that took years to discover, was to the question, *If self is real, it must need nourishment, so what is nourishment for the self?* I knew it wasn't air, food, and water, the nourishments for body and mind, but I couldn't see beyond that. When I finally realized what the answer was, I not only had a handle on the true nature of love, but a functional definition of love, and proof that love, as well as the self, was real. Love (loving energy) is the nourishment for the self.

I believe that love is one of the basic nourishing energies of life, just like air, food, and water, and not some romantic notion.[10] One that science has yet to "discover." Just like Democritus's atomos (which today we know as atoms, those tiny, invisible particles he postulated made up the universe), we have never been able to see love or loving energy. Just as atoms existed even though we could not see or measure them only two hundred years ago, not being able to see or measure the quantum energy waves that love is composed of does not make its existence, the energy I call love, any less real.

We have certainly all experienced the reality of love, such as when our mother smiled at us, when Dad hugged us, when a friend wanted to play, when our date really liked us, when our partner said "I will" and "I do," when our child said, "I love you." All of these experiences affect us in a very tangible, physical way. They served us (our body-mind-self) as beneficially as air, food, and water did and made us feel wonderful. These positive experiences gave us the nourishment our self needs. How do we know that for sure? Some part of us feels warm, energized, and nourished after having these experiences! The fact is that we feel nourished when we receive love, just like we feel nourished when we breathe in clean air, have a nourishing meal, or drink fresh water. I believe that what we call love is nothing more or less than the nourishment our self needs. Love when received and ingested behaves in our system as do all other nourishments. Love may not be tangible or visible, just like atoms aren't, but the way our body-mind-self reacts to both getting love and being deprived of love proves that love is real. This simple, practical analogy helps us to understand love is real and is needed as nourishment for self.

We would never discourage infants, children, teenagers, or even adults from asking for—demanding—air, food, or water if they were thirsting, suffocating, or starving to death. Life depends on those things. We are all very committed to physical survival, and we understand and encourage this commitment. When it comes to emotional survival, which depends on having the nourishment called love, it's quite a different story. By the time we're adults, we have become poor beggars on the bread line of life when it comes to love. We're afraid to ask for, and are often unable to get, the love we need, want, and deserve. And we're not much better at *giving* it to the ones we want to.

We all have felt warm and fuzzy, special and secure, and energized and happy. Sometimes we call it being loved. The warm-and-fuzzies are what we all want and need. But there are really painful feelings associated with love too, and we have all experienced those, as well. What is love if it can nourish us, make us feel warm and fuzzy, and yet also cause us to be in pain? How does this impact our understanding of the nature of love? What are the implications of this for psychology, psychotherapy, parenting, marriage, education, work, and relationships?

These questions puzzled me for years. Finally, the light bulb went on as I asked myself the following questions. Try answering them for yourself.

- Does food, a nourishment, cause us to be happy or in pain?
- Does water, a nourishment, cause us to be happy or in pain?
- Does air, a nourishment, cause us to be happy or in pain?

Having food, water, and air make us feel better than when we are without them. We need them for our very survival. Air, food, and water are vital nourishments for our body-mind. So, it is not air, food, and water themselves that causes pain, but only the absence of air, food, and water—the deprivation of vital nourishments for body-mind—which causes pain. This may be a simple fact that we all know, but it has powerful implications about the nature of love. It turns out that we react exactly the same way to the absence of love—deprivation of it—as we do to being deprived of air, food, and water. Think—is it love that causes us to feel pain or is it the absence of love that causes pain?

When we don't receive any of the vital nourishments we need like air, food, and water, we experience pain. When we don't receive love, we also experience pain. Is it possible that love is a vital nourishment, just like air, food, and water? Is it love that causes you happiness and pain? Think of when the absence of love hurt you as a child. I bet they were times like these: when Mom looked at you angrily, when Dad yelled, when a friend did not want to play with you, when a family member made fun of you, when someone you liked ignored you. Today, you may feel hurt when a spouse gets impatient, when siblings don't call, when a co-worker gossips, when a neighbor is inconsiderate, when your children don't appreciate your efforts. These situations all cause you pain because they are all examples of wanting to feel love present, and instead love is absent. These are all people you love but it is not love itself that caused you pain. It was the absence of the love that you wanted from them that caused you pain. When love is present you feel warm, energized, happy, and content. When love is withdrawn or not available, you feel emptiness and pain. Therefore, love is something we need and when we don't have it, when we are deprived of it, we suffer.

I told you earlier that I believe love is a real, vibrating energy, which can be generated by a human being and gifted to another, as well as graciously accepted or rejected. If love's presence or absence can cause extreme sensations like happiness and sadness, energy and weakness, it must be present or absent to have the power to effectuate this. If love is at times present and at other times absent, it must be a *thing*. If love is a thing, love must be real. Finally, as I have mentioned in earlier paragraphs, love behaves in the human being exactly like the known nourishments of air, food, and water. Therefore, love is real and nourishment.

Now that we have established love is a nourishing energy (the absence of which causes us pain), we must next ask, *What hurts when we are deprived of loving energy? Where is the source of pain?* It is clear to me that it is not my elbow, kidney, or any other body part that hurts in the absence of love. Although we continually refer to our heart (as in a *broken heart*), we seldom go to a cardiologist, like we do when we have a heart attack or a real pain in our heart muscle, nor is there ever a bypass operation performed for a broken heart. So, what hurts so much that some people choose suicide, go into deep depression, or suffer sadness for months? Again, I believe that the part of us that hurts and feels the painful absence of loving energy is the self.

I believe this is strong, logical, and experiential proof that 1) love, synonymous with loving energy, is real, and therefore 2) the self, which is nourished with loving energy, is also real.

Review

Love is a necessary nourishment. Love is either present or absent. The presence or absence of love causes the following: an increase or decrease of energy, a sense of well-being or lethargy, a feeling of joy or sadness. For all of these feelings and sensations to occur in a human being, it takes the presence or absence of real energy. These do occur in human beings, therefore love is a real energy.

That it is the absence of love that causes pain may now seem obvious, but in fact it leads us to a revolutionary new way of giving and receiving love. This thing we call love is a real energy—quantum, molecular, vibrating. Yes, it is invisible, and it is a necessary nourishment human beings consistently need. Love is uniquely the only nutrient that human beings themselves generate, rather than it coming from the environment (like air, food, and water).

Love—this unique, vibrating, living energy—is something we give and receive in different forms and amounts, such as the following:

A greeting	A smile	Encouragement
Understanding	Acceptance	Patience
Kindness	Teaching	Listening
Empathy	Acknowledging	Compassion
Supportiveness	Giving	A kiss
A touch	Graciousness	Gratitude
Being available	Intimacy	A hug

These and many more behaviors send love. We thrive on it and need an endless supply of it, as with the oxygen we continuously breathe.

2. A Developed Self Is Where True Power Lies

As mentioned, I believe that a fully developed self is the most powerful part of a human being. What do I mean by *powerful*? We all would like to be someone who touches, inspires, and motivates the people we meet in life. Often, we face situations where people are not touched, inspired, or motivated by us. We wonder what we could have done, what else we could have said. Why, we wonder, had we not moved them? We feel frustrated and helpless. We might even blame them for not responding to us.

When we love someone, we do not get frustrated, we do not get impatient. That comes from the mind and an undeveloped self. We might feel sad; by communicating our sadness (which comes from our heart-self) rather than our frustration (which comes from our mind), we can touch the other person's heart. I am using heart and self synonymously. Only touching one's heart-self is effective. It connects someone with the truth that they deserve to love themselves and it is only from that place that someone can do something beneficial for themselves. That is what I mean by *touching* another.

Touching someone means that their self has fully felt your love to the point that they realize they deserve not only your love but their own. It inspires them to look inward, to develop more awareness, to take action or to do something that will benefit many. The more developed one's self is, the more lives it touches, inspires, helps, heals, nurtures, and teaches.

This is true because a developed self realizes everyone has a self that is identical to theirs and is connected to them, connected to the whole. All selves need loving and they need to feel connected to other selves. This is like gravity—you can count on it anytime, anywhere. The developed self knows this and cares about all other selves. It no longer sees others in terms of color, religion, race, gender, nationality, or social position but as selves with similar needs to love and be loved.

I was looking for logical evidence that life span is in fact a three-stage developmental process, that each stage develops to a higher potential of a human being. I believed that it was important to prove that each stage, including that of a developed self, gives us greater control and greater power over our lives and over our environment. I believe that greater control and greater power develop as we move from using the body's full potential to using the mind's full potential, and finally by developing the self's full potential. I theorized that the potential of each stage of development was exponentially greater in power and effectiveness than the stage before.

The developed mind's potential and power is greater than the developed body's potential. We can immediately see that it gives us greater control and power over our lives and environment.

Let's compare the physical power of twenty of the strongest people in the world with a small, physically weak person who has a machine gun. A machine gun is a mental construct. It shows what the mind is capable of creating. We know that even though it's twenty people against one, it is still no contest. The individual with the machine gun can destroy all twenty stronger people and then some. The power of the mind always triumphs.

Think about all the tools the mind has invented to assist the body with doing tasks. Cars, trains, boats, cranes, telephones, television, machines that assemble with pin-point accuracy, not to mention flying machines. These accomplish feats which the body could never accomplish alone.

It is easy to see that the mind has exponentially increased human beings' control and power over life and the environment. This led me to contemplate how I can prove that developing the self's full potential can take us to an exponentially higher level of power and control over our lives and environment.

As you ponder this question, know that it took me over fifteen years to answer it. Yes, you read it correctly—fifteen years. I knew that if I didn't answer this question, I would doubt the strength of my theory of life span and my theory of self. If I did come up with the answer, I would have, with absolute certainty, validated the theory of self and therefore the effectiveness of my whole theory of human development. So, you can see a lot was riding on discovering the answer.

That piece of the puzzle finally fell into place. What is the most powerful thing a human being can do? Is it power as a display of strength, force, or speed? But there didn't seem to be any examples of the self creating anything like machines, which enabled the mind to transcend the power of the body.

I looked for those we all consider to be the most powerful people in the world, those we hold in highest regard. And it dawned on me. Their feats of power had nothing to do with physical or mental force.

I followed that line of thought and the answer was waiting, like a ripe, juicy apple ready for the picking.

The most powerful thing one human being can possibly do is to touch another human being. Touching us inside in a way that brings out the best, most compassionate, loving part of us. Touching us in a way that we feel fully connected to our own feelings and that of every other human being. Touching us in a way that moves us to action on behalf of ourselves and humanity. Touching us in a way that our personal self diminishes and our collective self takes on paramount importance.

We know about prisoners of war who chose to die rather than submit to the enemy. You cannot make people do something against their will. Yes, you can threaten people with harm and death, and most will succumb to the fear, but that is not *moving* someone—that is creating a malcontent who will wait for a chance to plunge a knife in your heart. And yes, you can bribe and manipulate them, but once you are discovered, they will loathe you.

Truly moving people takes a different power, one we all respond to. One that touches us deep at our core, actually touches the self in us, and inspires us to follow and do great things. One that makes us love not only the message but the messenger.

It is power of insurmountable dimensions that no physical or mental force can accomplish. Nothing has been ever invented that substitutes for this power. Moses, Jesus, Mohamed, Buddha, Gandhi, Mandela, Kennedy, King, Mother Teresa, and countless famous and nameless have done this. Men and women who have touched us and led us to greatness.

That, ladies and gentlemen, is the greatest power known to humanity, and it resides in the self, its potential waiting to be fully developed in each of us.

3. The Effort Scale

REGARD FOR ACCOMPLISHMENT

High

Medium

Low

Self

Effortless

Mind

Less Effort

Body

Effort

High   Medium   Low

EFFORT NEEDED FOR ACCOMPLISHMENT

FIGURE 1   Consider how a well-developed self performs effortlessly, and it is these accomplishments most fondly remembered in various cultural histories.

This graph illustrates the existence of the self. We will discuss the scale from two perspectives: first, by looking at the effort needed to achieve results using the body, the mind, and the self, and second, by looking at the level of regard to which people hold these various efforts. We will use the need to lift a heavy weight to compare body and mind.

1. Body

When using the body, lifting heavy objects takes a lot of effort, and we can't move them far if at all. How high a regard do human beings hold the moving of a heavy object, with all the effort involved? What impact does the effort have on our quality of life? Using the body to accomplish various goals and objectives is usually characterized by two things:

a) Low regard. These goals (like lifting, pushing, throwing, running fast, running far, climbing, seeing, hearing, shouting, swimming, jumping or any physical thing the body can accomplish without tools) are of a limited value. We don't hold the accomplishments of the body in very high regard, nor do we think these activities ultimately make a major contribution to the quality of human existence. They are all low on the scale of regard.

b) High effort. Most of the activities of the body are characterized by physical exertion, sweat, and strain, and they require the body to be in good shape. They are high on the scale of effort.

2. Mind

We notice it takes less effort to apply the mind to the same activity. To move a heavy object, we developed the lever, the inclined plane, the wheel, the pulley, the crane, and cranes on wheels. Our mind enabled us to use a lot less effort to move heavy objects a lot farther. Does this impact the quality of the human condition? Using the mind to accomplish various goals and objectives is usually characterized by two things:

a) Medium regard. By using the mind, we have taken all the things the body can and can't do (like fly, stay underwater for months, talk to someone thousands of miles away, see atoms, and the like) and developed tools that successfully enable the body to do them significantly better. Using the mind to develop tools is much higher on the scale of regard. We might claim that the quality of life has been improved by all the tools the mind has developed. Where would we be without airplanes or electron microscopes?

b) Less effort. Most activities associated with using the mind (like thinking, problem solving, predicting, learning languages, and mathematical computation) are characterized by less or no physical exertion, no sweat or strain. Advances such as cranes that can lift houses, high-speed trains and cars that can take us faster than our legs can, telephones and televisions that help us see and talk across the world, farm machinery that harvest an abundance of crops without breaking our backs, along with a million other inventions, are all examples of how the mind can be used to improve our quality of life. Higher regard, less effort.

Those who invented machines to supplement the strengths and weaknesses of the body, those who epitomize the use of the mind, are thought of with greater regard than those who exhibited physical power. We would like to emulate the success of inventors for the fame or fortune it might bring. Still, accomplishments such as developing the printing press (Johannes Gutenberg), electricity (Benjamin Franklin), the light bulb (Thomas Edison), penicillin (Louis Pasteur and Alexander Fleming), assembly lines for cars (Ransom E. Olds and Henry Ford), flight (the Wright brothers), and the telephone (Antonio Meucci and Alexander Graham Bell), while improving the general quality of life for many of us, didn't make us feel more human or closer and more loving toward other human beings.

I am arguing that—even though those who have invented those machines are thought of with high regard—comfort, ease, and even extended life are not synonymous with happiness and true satisfaction in life. Are we happier today? Do we have more inner peace and more satisfaction? Do we get and give more love? It is highly arguable that we are happier today, but if we want to make a case for that, we must ask, *Is our happiness attributable to our use of the mind that created these tools?*

The names of the people who conquered the world, who epito-mize the use of physical force, such as Attila the Hun, Genghis Kahn, Julius Caesar, Alexander the Great, Adolf Hitler, and Joseph Stalin, are generally not held in positive high regard but in negative regard. These people did not make us feel more human or feel a closer con-nection to other beings.

3. The Self

As impressive as the feats of the mind are, they still are not held in the highest regard by humanity. I am referring to the impact an act or invention has on the quality of our inner life—our happiness, our inner peace, our getting and giving love. The highest regard is reserved for accomplishments that seem to touch a part of us in-side—touch our hearts, our souls positively and move us to feel hap-piness and joy. Accomplishments that make us feel more human, feel a closer connection to other beings, come from the full development of the self.

Using the self to accomplish various goal and objectives is usually characterized by two things:

a) Highest regard. Using the self is usually characterized by a care and concern for the health, well-being, joy, peace, and satisfaction of other selves, not by sweat and strain or brainpower. When we con-sider Olympic gold medalists or the Nobel Peace Prize winners, it is easy to see who we admire the most. It is the people who win the Peace Prize. We sense that these people cared about us collec-tively and made our planet a more loving place to live. Just some of the people most attributed with this type of endeavor are Moses, Jesus, Muhammad, Buddha, Mother Teresa, Mahatma Gandhi, and Martin Luther King Jr. They are also the most revered and held in highest regard. Their actions brought us closer to feeling our own humanity and a human connection to others. The touching of another's self is the greatest power on Earth and can move humanity in ways that physical force, even intellectual force, cannot. We call these individuals *developed*—that is, they have become aware, they have used their awareness to create a loving vision effectively, and they are unconditionally loving. Those are exactly the qualities we strive to develop within each person using the Continuum Theory.

b) Lowest effort. Using a developed self is effortless. In using the body and mind, we can measure an effort output. It can leave us exhausted when we exert our bodies or our brains. When we use a developed self, there is no level of exertion. It comes from being—allowing ourselves to be. We are not using the body or mind in order to create more creature comforts or things. There is no sweat and strain or problem-solving involved. It takes work to develop the self. It takes work to develop the body and brain. But it takes effort when you use the body and brain. When you use the self, it has a quality of effortlessness.

A developed self is needed by human beings to achieve happiness, peace, and fulfillment in life. This cannot be accomplished by using body or mind alone.

4. Intuition, or the Inner Voice

Inner wisdom, sixth sense, discernment, inner voice, gut feeling, inner child—these are all terms we use to describe that sense we all have of something within us that is a source of guidance, awareness, and knowing that we either listen to or ignore. I believe it is worthwhile to look at what these universally accepted and used concepts may imply, based on experiential observation and inductive and deductive reasoning.

Hundreds of books have been written about all of these concepts. The constant references made to these concepts show a widely held belief in them. My explanation below, of why people believe in these concepts, is relevant to my theory of self. It will also give you more food for thought regarding their source, which I believe is the self.

Is it possible that all these refer to something calling to us from deep inside? Are there many separate entities inside each of us, or is it possible we are talking about the same thing? If it is the same thing, why do we insist on calling it so many different names? Why can't we just agree on one name? And when we say "same thing," do we mean "same source"? If we do, or if it is, what is that source of awareness, guidance, and knowing that we unintentionally experience?

We have all experienced a certain type of knowing that seems to have little to do with information we have obtained through reading, schooling, talking to friends, observing, or any past experiences we may have had. We meet a person we never met before. They are smiling and friendly, but somehow we just don't feel comfortable. Very often this discomfort turns out to be valid, turns out to have real basis, when something negative happens. If we didn't listen to that inner voice, we now realize we should have.

The business or social dealings you entered into (despite your gut feelings telling you not to) usually turned out to be a big mistake. Because I like people, I am also guilty of not having listened to that voice that said, "Something is not right." I have ignored it (magnanimously, I thought—after all, I don't know anything about these people, so why should I doubt them?), only to regret my decisions. Almost everyone I have ever spoken to has made similar mistakes of omission, having not listened to that voice from within.

What happened to a client a few years ago is something most of us are familiar with, and studies with twins corroborate this story.

One morning, she woke up and said she had the worst night of her life. Her head ached; she had not sleep all night. She felt there was something wrong with her daughter, who was going to school on the other coast. She called her immediately, and sure enough found her daughter crying. The daughter was very down and had had what she reported as the worst night of her life.

This instance is far from unique. As a matter of fact, it seems to be all too common.

We often explain this type of phenomenon by calling it a woman's intuition (thereby indicating that men seem to have less of it), gut sense (a feeling we all seem to get in the pit of our stomachs), sixth sense, intuitive cognition, discernment, feeling, hunch, idea, impression, suspicion. Roget's dictionary defines intuition as "the power to discern the true nature of a person or situation: insight, instinct."[11]

These terms and phrases are not based on one or two situations that one or two people experienced. They are based on an almost universal experience all people have shared from time immemorial. In mainstream human development and psychology circles, we tend to discount phenomena, we tend to discount phenomena we can't explain. Interestingly, we don't do that in other sciences—nuclear physics, astrophysics, biology, chemistry. Even if we can't prove it, we note it as a reality of that science. Astrophysicists have noted certain ways light behaves in space, and instead of discounting it have posited general relativity and the existence of black holes.

If we want psychology, philosophy of psychology, and human development to be more scientific, can we discount phenomena just because we can't see or explain it? I don't believe we can.

Next, we must ask ourselves from where this information that we only feel comes. Our intuition cannot be explained by simply calling it coincidence. The only way to explain these instances of knowing and connection is to simply admit that there must be a connection between people that we can't explain, see, or touch . . . yet. From a strictly materialist point of view, where there was no wire or physical entity connecting two people, there was no connection, and the pain the mother experienced at the same time her daughter was experiencing was just coincidental. But that is simply being silly. For the sake of pretending to be scientific, we will deny the limits of our understanding regarding finding out what in fact does connect us and inform us. By denying, we stop our search for the answer.

Because these experiences are universal, I feel it would be scientifically more honest of us to posit an explanation—a black hole—and pursue a line of questioning and research that may answer it. Which is what I did.

So let's get back to the theory. Because body and mind are electrical, quantum, vibrating energy fields, I believe the self is as well. We perceive the boundary of the body and we think that what we cannot contact, especially at great distances, we cannot know. The self, being an energetic vibrating quantum field, is not bound by the body. As such, it can connect with other selves, other energy fields, and have access to information, even from large distances.

In summary, our personal experience with the existence of intuition, inner wisdom, sixth sense, inner voice, gut feeling, inner child, and discernment all points directly to a source of knowing which I believe is the self.

Innate Human Abilities

Human beings have a number of innate abilities. Having an innate ability means nature has equipped us to do something without thought and without being taught. One innate ability we all have is the ability to learn how to walk. Watching the relentless efforts of an infant to stand and walk is enough to convince us of that. Yet, just as much as an infant strives to stand and walk, adults can interrupt, inhibit, or even damage that ability. Let's for example take an over-protective mother who decides to carry her daughter until she is two or three years old because she is afraid of her baby falling or touching germs. This behavior would interrupt and inhibit the development of the child's innate ability to walk normally. Imagine this same mother carrying the child until she was ten or fifteen years old. That would damage the daughter's ability to walk, and only painful rehabilitation could correct it. For centuries, some members of Chinese society bound female children's feet, believing that dainty feet were more feminine. The practice disabled these women for a lifetime. That is why it is outlawed in China today.

Another innate ability among the many we have is to talk. Even a century ago, the commonly held belief was that because infants couldn't talk, they were unintelligent and couldn't think yet. We didn't realize how developed their brains were for absorbing and re-taining knowledge. The only thing that wasn't yet developed was the muscles of the tongue, which would enable them to form intelligible sounds. This belief led to people using baby talk, imitating infant's sounds rather than teaching them, and in general not talk to their supposedly unintelligent children until much later. Although ulti-mately children did learn the language, the use of baby talk and lack of communication hindered the development of their brains and their grasp of language. Of course, we now know better. Infants are intelligent and capable of learning, so today every attempt is made to fully develop an infant's ability to talk and think as early as possible.

All children are born with the innate ability to love. Infants in-stinctively reach for, smile at, and hug their mother-figures, thereby giving and receiving loving energy. The ability to love is there at birth; however, it must be nurtured and fully developed so it can become unconditional in nature. It is developed by a combination of imitation and guidance, just like the innate abilities to talk and walk. Children learn to talk by imitation; the more we talk to them in complete, adult-like sentences, the more they will be able to express their thoughts in complete, adult-like sentences. The loving of others and the loving of oneself needs to be modeled the same way, consistently, so that a child can learn to imitate that behavior. As infants need for us to point to things and name them, loving behavior needs to be taught by modeling and by pointing to loving behaviors and naming them. Just like we lovingly correct a child when he misuses a word or falls trying to walk, we must correct his unloving, conditional behavior, lovingly. Most importantly, we need to model loving behavior in a consistent way. We want people to love us even when we make mistakes. Wouldn't it be nice for them if we loved them when they were less than perfect? I believe most of us love to love. We want to love. We are never happier than when we love. We need to love for our health and happiness.

As I said in the introduction, although the innate ability to love is there in every human being, for most of us it is damaged. Although some adults may be able to consistently give love, most are not. My father wasn't; my mother was. As a child watches parents walk and talk and wants to imitate them, a child watches and experiences how parents give, ask for, and withhold love. They end up imitating their parents' loving and unloving behaviors. As adults, they love in the same style they witnessed love being exchanged by family members (parent to parent, parent to child, sibling to sibling, parent to grandparent, and so on.) Sadly, the innate ability of loving, rather than being fully developed in a child, is damaged all too often.

Study: The Satisfaction Index

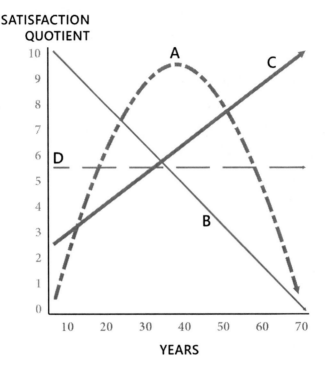

SATISFACTION
QUOTIENT

FIGURE 2   The *x*-axis represents some of the decades in a human life span. The *y*-axis indicates the level of perceived or anticipated satisfaction during those years.

I once conducted a survey that indirectly measured the level of anticipation with which individuals look forward to the coming years and decades. There was a total population of 288 people interviewed for this study with an age range of twenty-three to eighty-six, and to them I posed the following question: "If you had to draw life on a graph, from birth to death, and show where you believe life is at its peak (where it is at its most satisfying) and where it was at its lowest in satisfaction, how would you draw it?"

The results of this survey are included here as evidence because I believe that with the full development of the self comes real power, satisfaction, and happiness. I believe this stage of life should be eagerly anticipated and looked forward to. Instead, many people today are simply happy to be alive and healthy.

A. Dashed, bell-shaped line.

Seventy-three percent of the participants interviewed subscribed to this view of life and satisfaction. It starts at around one on the Satisfaction Index and peaks between thirty and fifty years and then steadily declines. Their age range was from twenty-three to six-ty-nine.

These individuals felt that there comes a time, somewhere between thirty and fifty years of age, when life starts to become a downhill experience. Irrespective of their ages, they were unanimous in not really looking forward to aging, and certainly not to the next decade. They felt being a child or teenager was too powerless because they had few choices, if any, and even the lack of responsibilities did not make the prospect more attractive. They also felt that the whole aging process, except for things like greater material wealth or security and higher career achievements, was still by and large a negative experience. They would have preferred to stay young, between twenty and thirty.

B. Solid, descending line.

Twelve percent of the participants interviewed subscribed to this view of life and satisfaction. It starts at ten on the Satisfaction Index and goes steadily down through seventy to eighty years of age. This group consisted of participants aged thirty to eighty-three.

Their notion was that life could not possibly be any better than when you and your every need are taken care of. You are also loved more than for the rest of your life. The rest of life after infancy and childhood is an ever-escalating series of struggles, disappointments, and responsibilities, ending with slowly eroding physical and mental capacity.

C. Solid, inclined line.

Ten percent of those interviewed subscribed to this view of life. It starts at around three on the Satisfaction Index and goes steadily upward as we age. This group was aged from sixty-five to eighty-six.

These participants reasoned that as you age, you tend to accept things the way they are. You let go of your dreams and become more realistic. Eventually, the kids grow up and leave, reducing parental responsibilities, and ultimately, you can retire and not have to work. They considered retirement the high point of life and worth looking forward to so they could do the things they always wanted—reading, traveling, watching the grandchildren, and so on.

D. Dashed, level line.

This group represented about five percent of the total interviewed. It starts at around five on the Satisfaction Index and stays there.

Participants who chose this were aged between thirty-five and seventy-two. Their reasoning went like this: life always has its ups and downs, so it doesn't really get any worse or better. Perhaps with age, we get to handle our problems more effectively. Life is what you make it.

Conclusions

Only ten percent of participants in the survey felt life was designed to get better and that aging was good because they have something to look forward to. Everyone in this group was already over sixty-five, so we might suppose they were rationalizing their situation, or perhaps this time in their lives was the best that they had experienced. This group looked forward to being grandparents, reading, traveling, gardening, and other things they wanted to do. I strongly feel that, as pleasant as those activities are, they are not synonymous with development and growth.

On the other hand, if we add up the other percentages on the graph, we can see that almost ninety percent of all people interviewed characterized life as a process, which after fifty or sixty years has more negative aspects associated with it than positive—a decline of body and mind, health issues, and financial dependency. For these participating individuals, their physical vitality and mental sharpness seemed to be more important than having free time. Simply doing activities that do not generate anticipation and excitement defeats the purpose and potential that life holds for us at the latter stages.

None of the groups considered that the most exciting stage of development, the one that has the greatest potential for achieving true satisfaction—developing power, effectiveness, mission, passion, connection, fame, and even fortune (all of which can stem from our becoming more aware and better at envisioning, communicating, and behaving unconditionally)—is the last stage of life after forty or fifty.

This last stage of development starts at approximately forty to fifty years of age and can continue until death! Within our developed self lies the answer to the question, *What is my life's purpose, and do I have all of the tools necessary to carry out that purpose?* Only when we come into the knowledge of our life's purpose and find ourselves engaged in pursuing it successfully do we come close to the satisfaction we are all entitled to. I believe in order to manifest true satisfaction, we must discover and achieve our life's purpose, and we can only do this if our self is fully developed.

Unrealized Opportunities to Further Explore the Self

I found one of the most interesting pieces of evidence for the existence of the self as I was researching intuition and insight. In the book *My Stroke of Insight: A Brain Scientist's Personal Journey* by Jill Bolte Taylor, PhD, a brain scientist speaks about her eight-year journey after a massive brain hemorrhage that wiped out her left brain. For eight years, she felt as if she was living in the "La-La-Land" of her right brain.[12] It was in some ways a wonderful experience for her. She writes about her experience of functioning without her left brain, without being able to sequence action or thoughts, without being able to learn or understand why any sequential action was necessary. But she doesn't seem to explain why, if she was so happy in the La-La-Land of her right brain and her left brain wasn't functioning, what part of her fought this eight-year battle to recover the use of her left brain. What part of her even had enough consciousness to decide that it wanted to fight this battle? Her only comment, but one that is dropped immediately, is as follows: "My scientific training did not teach me anything about the human spirit and the value of compassion."

Only very briefly is *the human spirit* referred to and implied as her source of motivation. Well, I asked myself, if so, wouldn't we all want to find out more about this human spirit? How does it function? How can we develop it? What nourishes it? How does it interact and relate to the body and mind?

Unfortunately, Jill did not take up that line of questioning. She was content to use the term human spirit and felt that she and everyone else knew exactly what she was talking about. I am certain, in her mind, no research is necessary, and the question of the existence of the human spirit, or self, continues to be unanswered.

NOTES

1. Richard M. Lerner, *Concepts and Theories of Human Development* (Mahwah, NJ: Lawrence Erlbaum, 2002).

2. Nicholas Rescher, *Studies in Quantitative Philosophizing* (Frankfurt: Ontos-Verlag, 2010), 20.

3. Joseph Melnick, "Editorial," *Gestalt Review* 5 no. 3 (2001): 161–166.

4. Thomas Mayor, "Hunters-Gatherers: The Original Libertarians," *Independent Review* 16 no. 4 (2012): 485–500. Consider also Maslow's hierarchy of needs.

5. Gardiner Harris, "Talk Doesn't Pay, So Psychiatry Turns to Drug Therapy," *New York Times*, March 5, 2011, accessed August 27, 2015, http://www.nytimes.com/2011/03/06/health/policy/06doctors.html?pagewanted=all&_r=2.

6. Jeffrey M. Schwartz and Sharon Begley, *The Mind and the Brain: Neuroplasticity and the Power of Mental Force* (New York: Harper Collins World, 2002).

7. In my experience, mental illnesses are not illnesses at all but rather people's reaction to trying to navigate life's problems without the proper tools.

8. Russell Howard Tuttle, "Human Evolution," *Encyclopedia Britannica*, last modified April 16, 2015, accessed August 30, 2015, http://www.britannica.com/science/human-evolution.

9. Thomas S. Kuhn, *The Structure of Scientific Revolutions* (Chicago: University of Chicago, 1962).

10. Barbara L. Fredrickson, *Love 2.0: How Our Supreme Emotion Affects Everything We Think, Do, Feel, and Become* (New York: Hudson Street Press, 2013). Fredrickson's research validated my hypothesis that love was nourishment.

11. *Roget's II: The New Thesaurus.* 3rd ed. Boston: Houghton Mifflin, 1995.

12. Jill Bolte Taylor, *My Stroke of Insight: A Brain Scientist's Personal Journey* (New York: Plume, 2009).

CPSIA information can be obtained
at www.ICGtesting.com
Printed in the USA
FFOW01n1149280417
34982FF